WAKING THE BONES

a memoir

Published by Piscataqua Press
A project of RiverRun Bookstore
142 Fleet Street
Portsmouth, NH, 03801
603-431-2100

info@riverrunbookstore.com
www.riverrunbookstore.com
www.piscataquapress.com

ISBN: 978-1-939739-60-5

Printed in the United States of America.

Cover Art: Sirarpi Heghinian Walzer

Visit the author at her website: www.elizabethkirschner.com

Waking the Bones

Elizabeth Kirschner

Elizabeth Kirschner
August 13, 2015

Rosalie,
May your writing
be blessed,
thanks

Elizabeth

~for my son~

We have careful thought for the stranger--
And a smile for the sometime guest--
But oft for our own, the bitter tone
Though we love our own the best.

~~Thomas Carney, 1900

"Enchanted Cottage"

CONTENTS

Prelude:
WITHOUT THE BITTER TONE
Kittery Point, 2013

Where do you live?

I live in a house on the water called Sea Cabin. I live in a house that my carpenter and I rebuilt. We rebuilt my house with silly putty and countless nails, with prana and plum lines, with fairy dust, plaster, and luxurious paints made from watered silks whose colors range from desert sage to cornflower yellow, from buckwheat gold to tangerine, ember red to a hallucinatory aquamarine.

How else did you and your carpenter rebuild your house?

We rebuilt my house with duct tape and desire, with screws and prisms, seaweed, shingles. We hung strings from the rafters to floorboards. We hung catgut strings, steel strings and the strings from all the pianos my piano-tuner grandfather ever tuned. We hung shoe strings, g-strings and the strings from a Stradivarius violin.

My carpenter and I pulled strings to restring my house. Now that everything has been hammered, laced and buckled into place, I pluck at these strings like heartstrings, or the feathers from a hen, many white feathers that feather me with otherworldly music. I'm feathered with the music of Schumann and Ahkmatova, with Rogers and Hammerstein, Dickinson, with Lawrence Welk and Li Po.

My Sea Cabin, was rebuilt in heaven, which is here, nine times out of ten. I, who am that woman my townspeople wonder about, have left other lands to get to my little house by the bridge. I have left 15 Debussy Circle and the Lock-Up. I have left the Kindercoffin, Tornado Country and the Berkshires.

So what if my townspeople wonder where I, that woman who lives by the bridge, came from? So what if I dragged a raft of gardens behind me--one embedded with Lenten roses and lungwort, turtlehead, loosestrife, foxglove? So what if I also dragged a litter of golden stars in my wake, tears green as emeralds, a bevy of priestly crows? Who cares when they hear such otherworldly music coming from my house morning, noon and night?

What music do your townspeople hear morning, noon and night?

They hear Beethoven and the Blitz Krieg, and the music of my fifty-eight Octobers. They hear fifty-eight gongs on an ancient temple bell whose coppery patina is covered with nubby layers of roseate mosses. The sound of my fifty-eight Octobers is in the heron's cry, the ping-pong of rain bouncing on my roof and the thunk of Mother's bat against my head. It's in the rip of my Patty Play Pal's limbs when Father tore them from their sockets, threatening to do so to me if I didn't comply and it's in the roar of the sea in my solar eardrum, love cries in the lunar one, and the heave-ho of the blood.

Where does your raft of gardens bloom?

My willy-nilly gardens bloom not only outside my house, but in my bookcases until the tale of Ophelia is entwined with Barbie, Sleeping Beauty with the Little Match Girl, Cinderella with Aphrodite. Here I keep sunflowers in birdcages, hydrangea in fish bowls, water lilies in mirrors where I see that the fairest in the land is always Grandma, not Mother.

Why isn't your mother the fairest in the land?

My mother isn't the fairest in the land because she didn't have time for beauty; she only had time to harm me.

When did she have time to harm you?

She had time to harm me, Little Bits, during Daylight Savings time, on the night before Christmas and after having a chocolate milkshake for lunch while reading the paper as Paul Harvey said, "Good day." She harmed me while the boomerangs in the avocado kitchen counter jiggled like worms, while the Shake 'n Bake chicken shivered in the oven and the cold contracted to spasm inside me.

What else did your mother have time for?

Mom had time to see spring in the ice crystals matting the pane that held her in, to love the dogwood blossoms, pale as bunny ears, and to go to morning Mass. She had time for eighteen holes of golf, the Pink Ball and time to sew, but her time to sew was not the same as the time to sow.

On what did your mother have time to sew?

She had time to sew on her Singer Sewing Machine, which was a huge, black mechanical wasp with gold markings, its needle, a giant stinger.

What else did Mother have time for?

She had time to stitch me. *A stitch in time saves nine,* she said, *a stitch in time saves nine.*

How did your mother stitch you?

She planted my hand under the Singer Sewing Machine until my finger bones wept. The Singer Sewing Machine went *rat-a-tat-tat,* as the needle bore in and out of me, like that of a furious acupuncturist. She ordered me to thank her for stitching me, but I refused.

Instead, I wrapped my bleeding hand in toilet paper, walked out the door, and stepped barefoot in spring snow melt. Beyond the pain that held me in, I smelled the pomegranate air, tasted the brandied sun. I began to sing, "Send in the Clowns" while I, Little Bits, walked out of the child I was to ghost her and make a blizzard in my brain, in order to remember to forget the childhood I was walking out of.

I not only walked out of the child I was to ghost her and reject her, Mother, too, rejected the child she once was. She rejected her dark, beribboned curls, her chiffon dresses, white kidskin shoes, small as a courtesan's with bound feet. She rejected her silver baby cup, ornate Japanese fans and hand-painted china dolls with limbs crooked as smiles. Because she had time, she also rejected her mother, Honora, who rang a bell for servants, locked her bedroom door nightly to keep out her drunk husband, a mother who insisted that we're the victims of victims, while praying on her glow-in-the-dark rosary.

What didn't your mother have time for?

She didn't have time to forget the tent where her mother's mother, Maria, her grandfather, Thomas Carney, and young brother lay dying during the flu epidemic. She didn't forget how her mother had been torn away from them, like a moth from the flame that draws her in, how her scream was heard round the world before it froze inside her. She didn't forget how huge hillsides were covered with tents reeking of sulphur and lemons, tents that were nothing more than stillborn wings palpitating with the uneasy wheeze of death breaths.

My mother's mother was dragged away from the tent where her own mother, father, brother lay dying because there is a time for sickness and for death. My mother's mother did not have time to grieve, for what is a child's grief but a whole world of sorrow packed in a penny whistle? My mother's mother was one more orphan in the orphaned world, who was visited by the angel of poverty because poverty always has time for orphans.

Orphaned and impoverished, my mother's mother had time to grow up and become a beauty. She had time to roll the sides of her hair up, twist them into a French knot, then powder her face with lavender talc until its silken transparencies glowed. She had time to become a Society's Child, to change her name from Honora to Eleanor because Eleanor was more elegant and beauty, not time, was on her side. Eleanor married my grandfather, Gilmore Estes, who wasn't impoverished, but from a proud, Southern family, who only believed in perpetuating family names.

Eleanor, not Honora, had time to beribbon the dark curls of her daughter, Eleanor Adelaide, to layer her in chiffon dresses, stiff as egg whites, to teach her to be a Society's Child, and not one more orphan in the orphaned world who was visited by the angel of poverty. She sent her to Charm School for her to become a debutante and be initiated into the Sorority House of Nightmares, until Mom rejected being a Society's Child, went from Eleanor Adelaide to just plain Ad and, at nineteen, married my father after meeting him in a bubble bar, he who courted her with baskets full of cold bouquets of bottled beer, not red, red roses.

Because daughters always have time to undo their mother's legacies, my mother did not have time to beribbon my dark curls, or layer me in chiffon dresses. Instead, she barbered my hair so short, kids taunted me, "Girl or boy?" Instead, I wore hand-me-downs and baggy dungarees. When my neighbor's son gave me a robin-blue party dress for my fifth birthday, Mom snatched it away from me. My party dress became a tent palpitating with the uneasy wheeze of death breaths and I heard my mother's scream go round the world until it froze inside me.

I had time to grow up. I had time to grow my hair out, long as a fairytale, to roll up the sides, then twist them in a French knot, like my mother's mother. I comb out its emerald tears, dragonflies and mysteries, its saffron scent, long, winding staircases and excessive eloquences. I tease out its archaic wounds, tinny archetypes, then powder my face with lavender talc until its silken transparencies glow.

Yet, I don't have time for beauty as my mother's mother did, or to be a Society's Child, nor do I have time to sew. I do, however, have time to sow in the gardens I dragged here on a raft and to cultivate, with painstaking rigor, my bookcase blooms.

Still, when I look into the mirror-poem of my mother and me, and then into the mirror-poem of herself and her mother, I see the pleats of one of those ornate fans, seven pleats, because all I am precedes me for not just two, but seven generations and all I am will follow me, not just for my son and his children's generations, but for another seven because there is, indeed, a time for perpetuating more than proud, Southern family names.

And so, I pay homage to my own, without the bitter tone, because I love my own the best. I pay homage to my cat and dog, to the coconut milk I drink from a yellow bowl every morning and the hot cinnamon tea I sip, day in, day out.

I sip hot cinnamon tea on this October morning while pondering the color of my soul. While pondering the color of my soul, I fill up with urine and yearning, only to empty myself of that urine and yearning. I see that my soul is blue and it's going to be half past evening all day.

Because it's going to be half-past evening all day, I pack up my Sea Cabin to carry on my back. I pack its specimen room where Mother is seed, black as caviar, in her father's left scrotum. I pack my garden room with its blood root pulled from the cool heel of my own father's foot and taste the iron of my mortality, its black flinty sugars. Because it's going to be half-past evening all day, I pack up my bone room, lunar room and prayer room with its green fountain gurgling with blood and laughter.

And then?

I carry my Sea Cabin on my back down to Fort Foster where the day is falling down, falling all the way down from sun-up to sundown. Here I enter the vast blue woods of my childhood and get lost at the bottom of my falling down day. Lost in the woods of my childhood, I see the layers of the roseate mosses, how they hold the velvet sufficiency of the skittish being who brought me here. I look for the milkman and my big brothers, then put my life down to study the undersides of butterflies as they fly in the lowest hierarchy of sky. I see that they're cloaked in saffron gowns, are battery-operated and quick as eye twitches. As my own eyes twitch, I realize that it's possible to let my story migrate, and I do.

While my story migrates, my life looks back at me and is a sad clown. That makes it time for my great-grandfather, Thomas Carney, to sing, without the bitter tone to that sad clown, who's just like the one in the picture in the bathroom where Father dragged me, after creeping on me. He creeped on me in my room, the kindercoffin, while biting my Little Bits ear. I bit him back. He got mad as a hatter, ordered me to be still, but I couldn't because of the pain from his creeping on me.

"That does it," Dad said in his businessman voice. He dragged me off the bed while I kicked as hard as I could. Into the bathroom we went where that sad clown picture hung. Father, like that clown, had a bulbous nose. He showed his tobacco-stained teeth as he said, in a voice big as a bassoon, "Little Bits, it's time to teach you a lesson." He filled the tub up with lukewarm water, put me in while his wrestler's hands bulged with purple veins. I kicked and kicked.

Outside the window, lightning bugs lit up the dark, hula hoops of lightning bugs, their tails, warm as glow worms. They lit up while Father's rage spread like a rash across his face. He shoved me under, held me there. Water stung my nostrils. I still kicked. I dirtied the tub. The filthy water got on the wallpaper's milkweed puffs while my lungs burned like fish bladders. Bits of shit got into my mouth. The kicking stopped. The numbness started. I went away, a tiny astronaut floating in outer space.

Now I float from space back into the vast blue woods of my childhood. There at the bottom of my falling down day, I say, "That was a long time ago," and then, I let time heal me. While time heals me, sheaves of roofs shift in the Sea Cabin on my back and all around the woods there are limbs larger than my Patty Play Pal's, which have fallen in the sword-flashing music lightning makes. I look up from the bottom of my falling down day to see a clearing, soft as a breast. Here plankton light swells from the groundswell and this is where my life now stands--astute, loose-jointed, bound by the beautiful failings of flesh.

What do you do next?

I pick my life back up. I let the butterflies, in their saffron gowns, be the fairies in fairytales, hear the black-capped chickadees go, *chick-a-dee-dee-dee,* in this, my land of old growth pines. The roseate mosses are not only sufficient as the skittish being who brought me here, they're also brash, fiery islands, which knead the soil into black gold. The woods of my childhood aren't blue anymore, nor is my soul--it's magenta and I have been found, not lost at the bottom of my falling down day.

What do you wish for now that you've been found?

Because I'm found, not lost, I wish to give my heart, without the bitter tone to my own, to the thous of my existence, which means I wish to give my heart to love, dear love.

Who are the thous of your existence?

The thous of my existence are the old pines, stalwart in silver curlicues of clouds under which Father used a razor blade to *cut, cut* angel wings into my shoulder blades. He *cut, cut* angel wings into me while saying I was no angel. Snow puffed, billowed leeward over a flat patina of water, still as knives in a drawer. Father *cut* my coarse cardboard flesh, tooling me, as though I were a hardcover book in which I'll come to write--*love is to pain what pain is to love is why is why is why*. I write in the stillness the water enshrines. In that stillness, my father remains entombed, because to be entombed was all that leered in the grimness he damed us to.

Who else are among the thous of your existence?

The thous of my existence are my family: *Maria, Tom, Gilmore, Honora.* My thous are *Lizzie Shields, Racehorse Charlie, Caspar, Edwina, my big brothers, my sister.* My thous are Donald and Ryan because family is the sweet, continuing sentence which makes me who I am. My thous are with me, like my own woman, fresh and dark.

They're my beauty, personal as a flower shipped in a box and their kisses taste of anise and chilly plums. I can never have enough of them. No, I can never have enough--of family, love, me.

As I leave the lostness of my falling down day, I become my own thou, my own dear me, mittened by inner light. I become the caesura, brief as wit, between this minute and the next, am the blue frogs roosting in the nearby marsh, like runes in sea brine.

I know that to be Kirschnerized means to get bigger with loss--big as a sheep pen, an ocean liner, a pyramid. When I get bigger with loss, all my thous enter my dear, Kirschnerized being, as does the eternity inside butterflies and the ferns with their laddered hieroglyphs.

When I get bigger with loss, my thous can't see the poison Mother milked into me from an emerald snake. My thous can't see the poison because they're intoxicated by the steam rolling out of that ocean liner, the pansied faces of sheep, the perfumes cloying the insides of that pyramid. They're intoxicated by my big Kirschnerized being, by me.

How did your mother milk poison from an emerald snake into you?

She held that snake by its throat, soft as the insides of my cheek, until poison bubbled like broth on its emerald lips. She then pressed those lips to my purple ones and said, *take this communion.*

What happened next?

I took my communion, then spit it out. I had a choice, so I spit out my communion. I've spent all of my mortal years spitting out my poisonous communion while looking for the milkman and my big brothers. I've spent years spitting out the broth of that communion, as well as the flinty sugars in the iron of my mortality. I've also put air into the globe, autumn into the cold tips of my toes and can sing a mile a minute.

What do you sing a mile a minute about?

I sing a mile a minute about the low charades the saints play, the apples pressed in applewood and my claustrophobic dead. I sing a mile a minute to the Little Bits that's me. I sing to bring the milkman and my big brothers back, to keep the day from falling down ever again.

Because I've extracted the poisonous communion from myself, I've grown strong in twelve different ways, which is almost as many ways as Stevens looked at a blackbird. Because I've grown strong, I can pick up my life, my big, Kirschnerized being, who's been newly freed by my own free hand. I carry my life and my Sea Cabin back home where I unpack all its rooms, from the garden room to the lunar one where I bath in oil and salt to fully soften my big, Kirschnerized being. Fully softened, my thous enter me for good.

What do you do then?

Buck-naked and freed by my own hand, I carry my life and its music to my dormer windows. I carry my life and its music to the windows, which a thousand winds have opened, like the silkily-scaled wings of lime-green luna moths. I also carry the child I once was, my communion and my claustrophobic dead because I have a choice. At the window, I breathe in the natural bare air, which is soft as the nubile flesh of that child's forehead. I breathe in bare air, feel the wings Father *cut* into my shoulder blades flex hard. My wings flex and thunder while I praise my Savage Maker, who is my inmost thou. My Savage Maker, my thou, always has time to love me. Here, at the windows of my life, which a thousand winds have opened, my Savage Maker loves me while my wings flex hard, thunder.

What happens next?

My magenta soul takes flight with a big *whoosh* sound. It flies to be with my Savage Maker, who is the milkman and my big brothers. My magenta soul flies in shrapnel grace to be with my Savage Maker and my thous. I then go to bed where I sleep like an open book.

It is a strange night. The milkman and my big brothers come to me for good, as does my magenta soul. All my thous come, especially my inmost one. I dream of a clearing, smooth as a breast, in the vast blue woods of my childhood. There, plankton light swells up from the groundswell to mitten me.

During this strange night, electric butterflies buzz on my ceiling, like mini-missionaries, only to become fairies. My thous send in Thomas Carney, to sing, once more without the bitter tone. “Don’t bother,” I chime upon waking, “I’m here.” Yes, I’m here, to sing, brief as wit, and isn’t that rich and isn’t it queer?

One:
A MEASURE OF MADNESS
2008-2009

All living things contain a measure
of madness that moves them in strange,
sometimes inexplicable ways. This
madness can be saving: it is part and
parcel of the ability to adapt. Without it,
no species would survive.

~~Yann Martel

"The Garden"

I.
ELIZABETH IN GA-GA LAND

After a long death, I start to come back. I start to come back even though I don't want to. Feeling shrink-wrapped, I come back, dimly wondering if I'm in the ER. I begin to hear things through my shrink-wrapped body. I hear my husband, Dr. Donald Frost, murmur my name, *Elizabeth, Elizabeth,* like the Jewish prayers he never learned. *Whir, whir,* goes my wispy breath while my mummified heartbeat *thunk-clunks* to the rhythm of my own rife blood.

In the ER, the steel edge of the hospital cart gleams by my bed. It's eerily cold and the ER floats--it's a space station turning over and over, and I float with it, a tiny astronaut. Am I an alien astronaut with an alienated mind, or is this another bizarre installment of "As the World Turns," with me in the role of Bertha Antionetta Mason?

The doctor, a conspirator, whispers to Donald, "How long has she been this way?"

My biologist husband answers, "I don't know. A neighbor found her at home. She's like this a lot."

I want to yell, "Am not!" even though it's true. I want to yell, "Am not!" but I'm too busy coming back. As I do, a drone glows in me like bees. The bees swarm in my hair, are tiny electric eels. They alight on my fingers and toes--one even lands in the bedpan the nurse slides under me.

"I'm peeing on the bee," I cry, "that makes me a do-bee, not a don't-bee."

My words hit deadpan silence. I go on, longing to be in Romper Room, not the ER.

"Don't you get it? I'm a do-bee peeing on the bee."

More deadpan silence, so I start to sing while peeing on the bee, "Do pee, do pee on the do-bee bee," I go, "Don't-bee, don't bee, the peed-on bee."

Eliz, Eliz, Donald starts to say, his voice, a mini saw sawing off my name.

I just laugh. "What don't you get?"

The nurse, doctor and my husband look stupefied, so I explain, "Peeing on the bee is good, but being the peed-on bee isn't."

No one smiles. The bedpan is removed in deadpan silence. The bees drones away in a golden swarm, like bronze topazes. I'm afraid Donald's voice will saw off my name again.

Instead, the doctor, who has handlebar whiskers, bends over me, asks, "Are you safe?"

I want to tug his whiskers, but don't. This is serious. "Yes," I say, dimly wondering how I, Kirschner, could kill myself when buck naked under a Jolly Green Giant johnny.

Unconvinced, the doctor asks again, "Are you safe?"

Boldly I answer, "Yes," even though it's not true.

I want the doctor to say, "Kirschner, don't kill yourself." Instead, he asks, a third time,

"Are you safe?"

"Yes, yes, yes," I say, like a lover sighing the name of her beloved. "Yes," I say, even though it's not true because I don't want to be put back in the psych ward. Who in their right mind would want to be put back in the psych ward? Who would want to toe the red line ten feet back from the locked door, the line we inmates aren't allowed to cross?

"Trust me," I say to the doctor and he does.

For now, this installation of "As the World Turns" ends. For now, I strip off my jolly green johnny, get dressed. Donald and I need to make a fast getaway--we hoof it out of the ER before the doctor can change his mind.

"Tra-la-la," I say, as we leave the hospital, "I guess it's just another slow day for the insane." I do a step-ball-change, even twirl a little because I'm not being rolled on a gurney into the lock-up. I twirl a little because the world has grown more expansive, expressive; the air tingles.

The light is bold. It has a big voice--*stir in the liqueur of my syrup.* It can be shared, like blood between kin. My breath *whirs* beneath its shining template.

"Look, Donald," I say, "the clouds aren't sharks anymore, not like they were earlier."

He glances up. "They never were sharks," he says, wearily. Has a measure of my madness migrated into him? Worse, has a measure of his madness migrated into me? Is this why I go mad? Or, has the hardness of living with me cleaved to him, like a blade behind his ribcage?

I continue, "It was worse when the clouds were baboons. They shrieked, *wa-hoo, wa-hoo,* so loud it hurt my ears."

Donald doesn't want to talk about cloud-sharks or cloud-baboons. Nor does he want to talk about the blade cleaved behind his ribcage. He just feels weary. Still, I want my husband, like the doctor, to say, "Don't kill yourself, Kirschner," but he doesn't. Is this because he's a biologist, not an MD?

Even so, after falling and falling for minutes, weeks, centuries, I've finally landed on solid ground, but for how long? Minutes, weeks, centuries? Will I, Kirschner, end up killing myself, or go to Ga-Ga land for good?

I don't know, I simply don't know. As we drive home, I try playing our favorite game. I turn to Donald, ask, "Who's your favorite poet?"

He's supposed to say, "Elizabeth Kirschner," really fast. Instead of saying, "Elizabeth Kirschner," really fast, he dishes out more deadpan silence.

I want to break that silence because it's shrink-wrapping us. I want to break that silence, say, *Pray tell, love, what hardened you? Why do you walk with winter, day in, day out, even though it's spring?* I want to say, *Please, love, forgive me, even though I don't know what I need forgiveness for.*

Instead, I note how the trees are greening. I see the party frills souping up their branch tips, hear the birds unfurling saucy songs.

When we pull into the driveway, my garden is popping with the fanfare of royal purple and gold crocuses. I turn to Donald, whose hands remain on the two and the ten of the steering wheel, even though he's stopped driving, ask, "Isn't it a yummy, spring day, so yummy it's edible?"

"Not really," he replies, from the corner of his mouth.

I'm tempted to remind Donald not to speak out of the corner of his mouth because I need him to make eye contact with me. I refrain. It's enough that I no longer hear thunder in the far side of my brain. It's enough that I'm no longer the cloudiness inside a child's marble and it's more than enough when our son, Ryan, runs out to greet me. I want to swing him so high, he'll forgive me. Instead, he swings me. I'm home for the week.

* * *

Ryan hasn't seen the old, falling down Maine camp, my Sea Cabin, where I've started to weekend. He wasn't with me when the realtor led me through a door at one end of the galley kitchen with its three peeling layers of linoleum, old floral wallpaper hanging like fly strips, blue cupboards on one side and a mustard-brown counter on the other with old, wood shelving below. "Lovely," I murmured, "just lovely" while the realtor oddly nodded.

We went into the living room with its moldy carpet smelling of rank flowers. There I kept my eyes glued on the three old six-over-six double-hung windows crookedly framing the pristine water beyond, flat as a hand mirror. The water beyond gleamed with the clarities that come after long sorrow. These clarities belong to the bright world I needed to go to, the one to which I now belong.

Maybe as I stared out those windows, my oar took its first tentative dip in those clarities, a dip so quiet it didn't make a splash.

The realtor took me up a set of stairs to the loft. There, the roof pitched so steeply, the front and back toe walls were only two-and-a-half-feet high. The ends of the loft were bookended by small windows, one of which had a window seat. The ceiling flagrantly bloomed with water stains shaped like strange amoebas.

I turned to the realtor. "Did you know that amoeba comes from the Greek word amiobe, which means change?"

Although this seemed relevant--wasn't my life about to undergo a sea change?--the realtor didn't respond.

I persisted, needing to prove I'd learned something from my biologist husband,

"They're microscopic unicellular protozoans of the rhizopodan order Amoebida." I almost added that my biologist husband lacked libido because he studied too many amoebas, but didn't. Would the relator appreciate the slant rhyme between libido and amoeba? I decided she wouldn't.

We ended up in the sunroom. There, by the crank windows, ten in all, I was pulled, once again, by the lure of the baptismal water beyond. I knew my writing desk would sit in its tidy prow and it does. "I'll take it," I said, then handed over a check to the realtor before she led me out through a second door in the living room.

We stepped into a gloomy lean-to consisting of three walls, two of which were old, cobwebbed storage closets. In them were tools rusted hunter-orange, broken lampshades the size of hat boxes, brooms, even a child's Little Bissell carpet sweeper. The front wall of this gloomy lean-to was enclosed by heavy, mildewed plastic that contained a yellowed "picture" window and a rickety screen door. A decrepit roofed-in shed with a dirt floor, it was tacked-on tackiness as depressing as the grand depression I was in.

"Just wonderful!" I exclaimed to the realtor, who looked a bit dazed as I climbed back into my car to drive home under a dreamboat sun. Then and only then, would I tell my husband what I had just done.

After sealing the deal with the realtor, that dreamboat sun, intimate as love, followed me, as did the seagulls, which were tossed up like hundreds of communion gloves. With their fickle attitude toward grace, the gulls followed me all the way home, as did the sun.

When I told Donald what I had done, I presented it as a proposal. "A partial separation," I declared, as if our long marriage could be partially separated, like curds from cheese, milk from cream. "I'll live there on weekends," I went on, "then come home during the week to take care of you and Ryan."

When Donald didn't flinch, I tacked on, "Don't worry, I'll take the dog."

Larka's tail went up, but he still didn't flinch. Instead, the air pockets between us chilled. Tauter grew the skin on his face while his thin upper lip became white as a nerve ending. His pupils contracted into two pin-sized cyclones. They might have sucked me in, but far inside, I felt the stir of wings, murmur of gull cry, soft as a rain shower. I also felt my husband's sadness, a sadness so old it overmastered him with an ice-capped isolation I couldn't touch, let alone heal because *love is to pain what pain is to love is why is why is why.*

As such, he walked right out of the kitchen to go sit in the living room, which was one of the cold, formal rooms in our home. Our house and our marriage were a toy theatre for Donald's cold, formal childhood. Its vestibule might as well have been a dressing room for the dead because we were in it, dressing and undressing, like pale mannequins.

AIone, I wondered: hadn't too much and too little been settled--my partial move to Maine, the exhausted air in the kitchen, a fate neither I or Donald desired?

Sighing, I stared at the fruit bowl. A wedding gift, it was rimmed with dogs chasing dogs. "It's a dog-eat-dog world," I said to Larka. Her eyes gleamed like watery onyx.

"Yep, it's a dog-eat-dog world all right," said Ryan. I wondered where he'd come from as he plucked three, then four peaches from the fruit bowl. He started juggling. He began whistling, too.

"How can you juggle and whistle at the same time?" I asked.

He simply whistled louder. I caught the tune. "This old man," I sang, "he played one, he played knick-knack on my bum," before turning to moon him.

He juggled the peaches higher, faster. I sang some more, "this old man, he played two."

Ryan finished for me, "he left dog-do on my shoe." He then exited the kitchen, still juggling the peaches.

*   *   *

Soon after, long after, I start to weekend in Kittery Point. After one such weekend, I finish the drive back to 15 Debusssy Circle, enter the house with the dog. As soon as I do, demons blitz me, attack full throttle. Attacked, these demons buzz, like a horde of fever bees--or are they pit-bullish, teeth-baring gods? Demons or gods, they shrinkwrap me with their red-and-black reptilian wings. Amid their seismic drone, I grope for my meds, my superglue for the brain.

As I grope for my meds, my demons furiously back off. Grief, with its ungodly underbelly, despair, *cut, cuts,* into my heart. I keen loudly, like an animal whose throat's been slit. Tears, too, a great gush. I'm going away, dying to die.

Dying to die, I grope for my meds. I want swallow them all, go away for good.

Instead, shaking as if palsied, I grip my cell phone, try to make calls. Tears insinuate my vision as I push the wrong buttons, again, again. Who can haul me out of this?

Finally, I reach *a* voice, the voice of *a* doctor in Urgent Care. I'm so far gone I can only sigh, *die,* while weeping, *die.* Then I drop the phone.

Soon after, long after, my next door neighbor arrives. By the time she reaches the house, my shrink-wrapped body can't get off the foyer stairs to let her in. The dog barks, frenetically. Hanni pounds on the door, The dog barks some more, but I can't move.

Hanni calls Donald at work. When he arrives, the only word I can mouth in a mute voice is *hospital.* He goes into action as he has done so many other times because before starting to go to ga-ga land, I had hundreds of seizures for seemingly hundreds of years.

Donald calls my doctors, gets permission to put me in the psych ward where I've been too many times before, toeing the red line.

Can you make it to the car? he asks.

I shake my head, *no.*

Should I call an ambulance?

Also, *no.*

He asks again. This time I can't respond. Slowly, ever so slowly, he and Hanni drag me to the car, muscle me in. As my eyes stammer closed, I see that the clouds are sharks. The clouds are baboons. *Wa-hoo, wa-hoo,* they screech, so loud it hurts my ears. They drag claws down the boat runnels of my chest. I hear my flesh rip, feel my own rife blood as it's shed. Into my long death I go.

My shrink-wrapped body stays in a long death for minutes, weeks, centuries, until I start to come back. As I come back in the eerily cold ER, I float, a tiny astronaut with an alien, alienated mind, wanting only to go away for good.

Instead, I say, "Yes," when the doctor asks, "are you safe?" Instead, I say, "Trust me," and he does.

Soon after, long after, I pack up my stuff. I haul car loads up to the camp in Maine, shredded by a fate neither Donald or I desire. I'm shredded even more by leaving my fifteen year old son behind. Shredded, I leave Ryan behind because I need to save him. Saving him means saving me. It's that stark. What could be starker--a crazy mother, or a dead one? I choose life.

II.
DONALD AND ELIZABETH ON VACATION

Perhaps the fate neither Donald or I desired had been birthed, whacked and wailed into being long before I rented my Sea Cabin in Kittery Point. Maybe it'd been settled on some somnolent summer night in our cottage in the Berkshires as we shuttled into sleep, enclosed by the flask of a fluted dream which tippled into us the tremolo of shriek owls. That fate may've been settled when the first stills of attraction grew lambent between us--like a slow freeze on hot tarmac--or in the wafting shadows of our unshared childhoods. In us, it turned one eye inward, the other outward, pickling our vision, while our fate grew surly, powerful as pestilence. This pestilence divided all that had bound us together, into grievances, spoken or not.

While vacationing in Bequia--an island off the coast of Venezuela--our undesired fate happens to come along for the ride. It fully engages us. Divisive, this fate deftly folds our inward eyes so far in, they're tiny pocketbooks, even as our outward ones are cast way beyond ordinary vision. Our outward eyes are cast onto the fronds of palm leaves, delicate as fallen eyelashes. They're cast onto the spears of light lancing the placid seawater and across the pinked glints of sand warming our Northern toes. Our outward eyes even take in the opulent banquet the world harvests anew each day. In that banquet, we see hoodlum blossoms, a silk window of sky. We listen to breezes parting the waves, to cockatoo cantatas, dissolvable as grace.

While our fate kneads us, Donald and I work hard to have fun on vacation. One morning over coffee, I look into his eyes, as they transit into vacant, cellular rooms furnished by the ghost who fathered him. Lost, not found, in these cellular rooms, I pip, "Let's go to the Turtle Sanctuary. Don't you want to meet Orton King, the turtle-hunter turned turtle-savior?"

My biologist husband rolls his vacant eyes, replies, "I'm overheating and sweating like a pig."

"You're always overheating. Let's go," I cry, "let's rock that Turtle Sanctuary."

"If you insist," Donald says, as he stands up to tie his tank top round his head to keep the sweat from getting into his eyes, eyes which once played upon me with sexual wonder. My own--tiny, alert--flash.

Off to the Turtle Sanctuary we go. Here, Orton King, the turtle-savior, walks us round a series of jellybean-shaped tanks, which hold the hatchlings until age three when they're released back into the sea. These turtles, these Hawksbills, are endangered. This endangerment feels crushingly close--it's the heritage pertinent to all species, even that unprotected one called marriage. It's also in the rogue, runaway genes laddering us.

Orton King drones on and on about the Hawksbills' declining numbers, egg poachers, traders in their shells, until I say, "Look, the turtles' mouths look like funny beaks. Do you think that's why they're called Hawksbills?"

"Yes, Ma'am," pipes in Orton. Donald doesn't seem to be listening as he's busy plucking, then eating his whiskers.

"Ah," I go on, "their carapaces are heart-shaped. I want one for Valentine's Day." I rarely even get a card, but I keep hoping.

"Lady," Orton warns, "they're not for sale." Donald's still plucking and eating his whiskers. He's also overheating.

I almost blurt that my biologist husband should poach a turtle because it might save us. Instead, I fix my tiny, alert eyes on Donald, say, "Maybe you should swim with the baby turtles. Do some research on turtle talk."

Donald rolls his eyes again, but I go on, "I know, I know, you're overheating and sweating, but I can't help but think about how these turtles only eat sponges. I don't think I could eat sponges day-in, day-out, especially kitchen sponges."

Donald asks, "Can we go now?" It's a question that edges on command.

"Sure, sure" I say, "but I have to tell you these turtles are luckier than the one I won in the Turtle Race at the Fun Fair back in grade school. I carried him home in a Chinese takeout box, set him up in the plastic tank with a blue umbrella." I pause, then add, "I think he died out of plain boredom, or froze because Mom didn't believe in central heat." Donald yawns.

"A pet funeral is one thing," I continue, "but when it's twenty below out without the wind chill factor, a turtle funeral isn't just pathetic, it's downright grueling."

I'm on the verge of saying the cakewalk was even more fun than the turtle race, but my husband is plainly bored, so I drop the subject.

That evening finds Donald and I hunched over our dinner plates, shawled by the lilt of sultry breezes which baste our arid temperaments. We're still working while on vacation and as we do, the candle on the table flickers, swan-like, goes out. Its smoke is char and my lips--purple, Lenten--flower from the wine we're drinking. Donald's crease into a pucker, like petals that only know how to close when common evening comes. I long to open those lips, tongue his tongue.

I decide to try for conversation. "Don't you think it's funny that a restaurant called *The Devil's Table* has a Swedish chef?" I ask before adding, "I wonder if they serve Swedish meatballs, or Devil's food cake? If so, I wish Ryan were here because he loves them both."

"Elizabeth," Donald says, "you're slurring your words." This phrase is one of his favorites. It hits me like a hot flash. He goes on, embarrassed, "Even the taxi driver commented on your drinking."

I push my wine glass away, say, "Sorry," with downcast eyes. My inward one weeps while the outward one refuses to look at Donald because if it does, his own eyes will chip me. In the warm evening, I start to shiver, quiver and go out, just like the candle.

Donald heaves a breath or two, pushes away his chair. He stands up, says, "Go, just go." His hand waves, like a flag. I surrender, obey, even though we haven't eaten. We don't even know if the Swedish chef serves Swedish meatballs, or Devil's food cake, but it doesn't matter because fate's fabulous appetite has just taken a meaty chunk out of us.

I trail Donald as we leave, falling behind him, falling very much behind him, his backbone stiff as a poker. Suddenly, I remember what I drink to forget--how Father once rammed such a poker up my anus. He branded me with the garish sear of my own burnt flesh. Barely five years old, the smell of burnt charcoal, seared with my own feces, engulfed me.

That smell engulfs me now, is staggering. I stagger after Donald, trailing way behind him. I trail him to where the taxi driver waits for us, the one who has commented on my drinking. The driver helps me into the truck bed--all the cabs on Bequia are trucks with open benches. I sit on its cracked blue bench, trying to fold in each of my thin bones, like the spokes of an umbrella.

As I fold in my bones, I remember a line from a poem, *It's raining marvelous women's voices.* Because it's raining women's voices, a nighttime sun-shower of women's voices, I hear Honora's voice streak down. I hear Edwina's, Lizzie's, Aunt Rita's, even my own voice streaks down. For a moment, this nighttime shower of women's voices, cleanses me. It cleanses me of the smell of burnt charcoal.

Cleansed, I forget to tell Donald what I drink to forget. Instead, I ask, "Don't you hear marvelous women's voices raining down?"

"No, not exactly," he replies, speaking out of the corner of his mouth.

"Blue raindrops," I murmur, "beautiful women's voices marvelously raining down," I murmur.

"Elizabeth," Donald says, "it's not even raining," yet I'm fixated on the heavens from which these women's voices rain down. There, the night flickers its onyx secrets. While these secrets flicker, the taxi driver speeds down quirky, bumpy, fast-turning roads. In the heavens, the Milky Way blooms with noiseless fireworks. These fireworks appear, disappear, are exotic. For a moment, I taste a bit of the sweetness that once sweetened Donald and me, like chocolate served with two round oranges.

We arrive at our hotel, a white hotel. At this white hotel, I long for that chocolate, for two round oranges. I long for a walk, a conversation, while the night still flickers its secret, onyx charms, but the taxi driver is getting out the truck to help me down. I then notice: my backpack is gone.

I pause for a second, long as a closed eternity, before whispering to Donald. "It's gone."

"What's gone?" he replies.

"My backpack," I answer, "it must have bounced out of the truck on the way back to the hotel."

"What's in it?" he asks. His voice peels me, like the rind of one of those oranges, the ones we'll never have, nor the chocolate, a walk, a conversation.

Peeled, I let out, "Passport, credit cards, plane tickets."

"Elizabeth" he says, "living with you is a crisis, just one crisis after another."

This, too, is among Donald's favorite phrases. It scours me, like the steel wool pad Mother scrubbed my cheeks with to get my dirty dish rag soul clean. I stand still, mute. I want to go away, be a tiny astronaut, or better yet, don my skeleton costume, the one I wore to spook off Mother and Father. Instead, Donald's breath scours me.

"Get in the truck," he says. I obey.

He tells the driver to backtrack our steps. We search everywhere for my backpack. We search the Devil's Table. We search outside the restaurant, in a metropolis of tree roots, and under stones, flat as pancakes. We search mailboxes, the tall envelope the night envelops us in, even the sultry breeze which bastes us. We search low, search high. We search all the notes in the musical scale until we get stuck in C minor. We don't find my backpack. Donald's breath scours me again.

The Caribbean night is turning into a perfume too expensive to own, let alone wear. I start crying. My tears are drops of Chanel #5, White Nights, Cashmere Mist. My tears are drops of Angel Trumpets and Euphoria, but I reek, once again, of burnt charcoal seared with my own feces. I rub my arms to get off the reek--my hands, small dark erasers.

Back at the hotel, Donald goes into action, plays telephone. He cancels my credit cards, calls his sister back home where she's caring for Ryan, asks her to look for copies of my passport. I stand stiff as my Patty Play Pal before Dad tore her apart, limb by plastic limb. He tore her apart in my Playhouse where he insisted that this was what he would do to me if I didn't comply. The limbs fell like plastic socks.

Donald and I go up to the hotel room in stone-age silence. His heavy sighs scour me as I flounder on the bed under mosquito netting that sizzles in the heat. I cry more, pitifully so, still stuck in C minor. A whistle goes through my C minor cry while Donald starts to seethe. The seething is hot lava, sears my cold flesh where it hardens, threatens to bury me.

That night, as Donald seethes and lava covers my body until it hardens, I keep crying my expensive tears until I slip, briefly, into sleep where I bask, even more briefly, in a dream. In it, I open huge, dormer windows, let in bins of natural bare air. Window after window opens, like the wings of dressy, green luna moths, as I stroke the bare air, nubile as an infant's forehead. The windows keep on opening, even after I awaken. They open like the lifetime I haven't yet arrived at, the one which is in the bright world that is my Sea Cabin.

When I awaken, in the middle of the night from my fitful sleep, I hear the sound a guillotine makes as it drops. Moonlight glints on its blade as it falls--*whoosh*--vertically through the bed. The sea sweeps over the balcony, floods the room, stranding Donald and I on our separate islands. These islands, so unlike the pillow ones Ryan and I played on when he was little, strand us, but it will be me who's swept away for good.

After being stranded all night, we get up. The sea is quiet as a music box to which someone has thrown away the key. We get up in bodies that are waterlogged. I hear the liquids slosh around as we go about dressing in Stone Age silence. I put on my chemise. For a moment, I think it's bleeding. I almost blurt, *My chemise is bleeding,* but such an outburst would only result in Donald saying, "you're crazy," which I already know.

The chemise chaffs me as we go down to the dining area in our waterlogged bodies. We sit down for breakfast, only it's not two round oranges served with chocolate, but waterlogged French toast. While our body fluids slosh, we drink down lukewarm coffee.

Without looking up, Donald says, "the marriage is untenable."

"What?" I ask, "Did you say unbearable?"

"Whatever," he replies with a shrug.

Nothing more is said about our untenable, unbearable marriage, not even after it's announced over the island's P.A. system that my backpack has been found. Nothing more is said about our unbearable marriage, even after we retrieve my backpack, its contents intact. Nothing more is said about our marriage all the way back home from the vacation we've worked hard on.

All the way home, I hear the guillotine go, *whoosh.* On the ferry where there are gypsies with gold teeth and children like thin ghosts, it goes *whoosh* through the bench Donald and I sit on. I bend forward to speak to these ghostly-thin children.

"Where does the moon come from?" I ask.

One child points to the wishbone-white horizon. "There," she answers.

"Yes," I say, "but does it sleep in the water during the day?"

The children look at each other, baffled.

"Do you think sea monkeys play in the moon's wishy-washy rays?" I ask.

They smile.

"Maybe puffer fish and magic carp swim in its navel. Or do you think glow worms snooze in its loony ears?"

The children giggle, then turn back to the wishbone horizon. I want to make a wish on that horizon. I want to wish for my husband and I to live happily ever after, but before I can, it vanishes.

As we step off the ferry and onto to the dock, I hear another *whoosh.* During the two flights home, above clouds wispy as daisy petals--*whoosh.* Even in the cab from Logan Airport to our Newton home, *whoosh.* Each *whoosh* further severs our ability to talk about our marriage and weeks later, when I put the deposit down on the camp in Kittery Point, our silence is signed and sealed.

Soon I'm driving up the highway to weekend in Kittery Point. I drive under a sky full of gulls, like tiny white saviors. Their murmurs anoint me with love cries and their fickle attitude toward grace.

In the distance, Donald is closing the door, slowly turning away from me as he has for months, years, centuries. It's his genius to turn away. At the dinner table, when I whispered, "I have to go," he silently laid down his knife, lifted the paper, opened it, let the print stain his fingers, the ones that have not touched me for months, years. Because my husband hasn't touched me for so long, I want to whisper, *o my beloved, where are you?* but can't, don't, won't.

One day after weekending in Kittery Point, I return to Newton, enter the house where my demons attack, full throttle. They attack until I fall into my long death. I fall and fall, only to slowly come back. I come back in the ER, longing to go away, for good. Instead, I pack up my stuff. I pack up, leave Ryan behind. I leave Ryan behind to save him from myself. Saving him means saving me. What good is a crazy mom, or worse, a dead one? I choose life.

III.
THE MOTHER SHRINE

In my Sea Cabin, I unpack. I unpack suitcases full of bones--ghost bones, bird bones, funny bones. I sing as I unpack saffron bones and the bones of Queen Elizabeth, dead for five hundred years. I sing as I hang fire bones in closets, tight as caskets. I hang lapis lazuli bones in these closets where they're adorned with lace, lemon meringue and scarves billowy as the acres of water beyond my windows. I adorn xylophone bones with my grandmother's piano shawl, the leafy trellises of terza rima and patches of my songs, long as windy corridors.

My songs are rehearsals in truth. As rehearsals in truth, they skip to the loo before going down on bended knee, just to up-flutter like doves. My songs leaven my Sea Cabin until the rafters swell and the floor joists bow out like hulls.

My songs wake the bones in the attic I do not have, the cellar never dug. They're waking the bones in the gardens I dragged here on a raft and the ones in my bookcase blooms. They're even waking my bones, until a succulence is drawn, like butter, into my nervy roots. By touch, I transplant my succulence into the garden roots, which grow milky, then turgid. These roots push through roofs of dirt, crushing the last ice crystals matting tendrils delicate as glass threads, yet visceral as the eye muscles that contract and expand my vision.

My vision contracts, expands by tunneling into feeder roots which then tunnel into those embedded in my words, words I also plant by touch. My vision--like sunlight, like stars, like char--grows my desktop garden where I plant and exhume. I plant seaweed, exhume snow. I plant double-hipped rainbows, exhume death, smelling of limestone and desire. I plant the elements the night hides in, exhume hoodlum blooms.

When not growing my desktop garden, or tending my bookcase blooms with painstaking rigor, I sleep. While I sleep, waves lift from the water beyond my windows to caress me. The waves caress me as the blue raindrops of women's voices--Honora, Edwina, Lizzie--marvelously rain down. They caress me while women's voices rain down to sift the grit from my inner transparencies. When I wake, I'm awash with these transparencies, with audible light.

Awash with light, I cross three bridges and three states to go see Ryan. Weekly, I cross three bridges and states to go see Ryan because by seeing him, I save him. By saving him, I save myself because I choose life.

Weekly, I go see Ryan, but all too soon, the spring of my abrupt departure swandives into a summer, lenient as prayer, which then passes, allowing autumn to arrive, like a burden that levies a certain tax. Weekly, I still go see Ryan.

My son bops out to my car. When he gets in, I want to say, *It's honky-donkey time.* I want to say, *bim-bam doodle, I'm in love with a noodle*, or, *laugh in giraffe, get funky in monkey,* but he's too old for nonsense. Instead, I say, "Hi honey, how are you?"

"Fine, Mom," he replies, "but can I show you something funny on my computer?" I hesitate. I haven't been in the house since the partial separation turned into a permanent one, less than six months before.

"Please, Mom," he says, "it's really funny."

"Okay, okay," I reply while getting out of the car. We walk down the granite-and-slate walkway, the one I designed. We walk by the gardens I designed. I see that Donald's been pruning our little family of rhododendrons, hard. Piles of branches are scattered around them. Our rhododendrons have been cut back to bare nubbins. They'll never recover. Will we?

"Poor things," I say.

"I know," replies Ryan. "They look like stick people.

"Worse," I go on, "they look like starving stick people." Do we look like stick people, too?

"Come on," Ryan insists, as he grabs my hand, takes me inside.

Excited, he pulls me toward his room, yet in order to get there, we have to go by the bedroom Donald and I shared for so long. We have to go by the conjugal bed where we tinkered until we winked our son's first cells into being.

I can't help but look. With the blinds closed, the room looks morgue-ish, brightened only by the duvet cover on the bed, the one I chose long ago. It has hundreds of colors whirling in hundreds of flowers, wild as a flying cosmos.

I gasp. There on my side of the bed, atop the periwinkle pillows are Ryan's stuffed animals. They're piled into a Mother Shrine.

I stare at the Mother Shrine, the one designed for me with my boy's stuffed animals.

"What's up, Mom?" Ryan asks.

I cough back tears. "Oh, nothing," I say, "just thinking."

"Do you want to play Islands?" he goes on.

"Islands? We haven't done that in years."

"So?"

"I thought you had something funny to show me on your computer?" I ask, hopefully.

"Nah, I'd rather play Islands."

I want to say, *but you made a Mother Shrine on my side of the bed.* I want to say, *You made me a Mother Shrine, even though I left you behind,* and, *You made me a Mother Shrine--did I earn it?* but Ryan is already putting the pillows on the floor between the beds, all the pillows, except for the one upon which his stuffed animals are enshrined.

"Okay," he announces, "the pirates and sea monsters are trying to get us. We must hop from island to island to the lifeboats without falling into the treacherous sea."

I want to say, *but I've already fallen into a treacherous sea.* I want to say, *I've been swept away by that sea,* and, *The sea monsters are devouring me,* but I just leap. "Down with the pirates!" I yell.

"Ye nasty pirates, be doomed!" Ryan calls out as he leaps from island to island. For a moment, I think he's six or seven again, not fifteen going on sixteen. For a moment, I think I'm six or seven again, not fifty-four. I think this until Ryan leaps onto the lifeboat, the conjugal bed, the one he has enshrined.

"The nasty pirates have been conquered!" he cries. "Woe to

them, yea to me!"

I stare at the stuffed animals. They're curled like babies around their mother's teats.

"Yes," I say, quietly, "woe to them, yea to you," while remembering how my own nipple, hard as a tuber, had warbled into my son's mouth, moments after he was born.

Woe and yea, indeed.

*   *   *

Later, at the restaurant we always go to, Ryan assesses the rolls, which have arrived in a black basket as I say, "Words are the hands with which I touch the world."

Ryan simply nods as he tears into a roll, then dips it in oil. This is what we do--break bread, share.

"Right out of the oven," he proclaims. His eyes are a dedicated blue, his hair ginger-colored.

"A rare treat," I respond, while he slips two rolls into his sweatshirt's kangaroo pocket, like hot rocks meant to be hand-warmers.

If we break bread, share, we also break words to share. Ryan says, "I just wrote an essay titled, *A Hands-on Investigation of Hands.*"

"Sherwood Anderson," I reply, naming the author of the story he's referring to.

"*Winesburg, Ohio,*" he goes on, the title of Anderson's book.

"In the Heart of the Heart of the Country," I say, quoting yet another story, but by William Gass because that's where I grew up. "I read Sherwood Anderson in college," I continue, "I was down in the library stacks where I always studied. The stacks were sickly green, like a submarine. I threw the book across the room when I finished it. That's how powerful it was."

"Wing Biddlebaum was tortured because of his hands," Ryan goes on, "he touched his students in order to impart in them an intangible force, the force of dreams and possibilities."

"Excellent," I reply, "great connection and what a name, Wing. I'd love to be called Wing," then repeat, elaborate, "Words are wings I plant by touch."

"So that's what you do," he says, quietly.

For a moment, I remember how Donald once planted me with his touch before that touch shriveled, like a penetrating nerve slipping back into his hand. Was it because the force of dreams and possibilities no longer existed for us?

I give Ryan a poem, one I recently wrote, a found poem created out of the flash fiction he'd given me the week before.

He reads the poem silently. When finished, he looks up. "The best part is 'Construct a seed. Revolt!'" His eyes flash, like water, like minnows.

"I think so, too," I reply.

All too soon, we go out into the autumn darkness, which is constantly falling these days. Soon I drop him off at his father's house, the one I couldn't drag him away from, like my raft of gardens. I couldn't drag him away because transplanting his tensile, virile roots, would've put him into shock. Instead, I transplanted myself back to where I'd lived, for over a decade, before I met Donald. I transplanted myself back and even though my roots bleed tears, they somehow water Ryan's because I choose life.

IV.
MUSIC IN A DISTANT ROOM

When I'm not crossing three bridges and states to see Ryan, or tending to my desktop garden and trundling in waves of sleep, I'm shopping. Because I'm shopping when not visiting Ryan, or embedding words in loamy roots, it becomes my forte. I work clothing stores the way a criminal works a crime scene. I work them the way my cousin, Gil, a three-times felon, knows how to rob a bank, is behind bars, incarcerated, as I've been incarcerated and will be again, but behind the red line in the psych ward, my home away from home, my getaway, I who go mad from remembering a childhood I remembered to forget.

In one such shop, I'm rifling through the clothing rack, running my fingers through different fabrics--silks, velvets, cashmere--listening to the tags rustle, fondling tender buttons. A blue dress flies off the rack. I hustle it into the dressing room, my throne room, strip off my black beaded skirt, wrap blouse. The blue dress slips onto to me like my little helper apron with its cake frosting flounces, or the party dress Mother snatched away from me when I was five. Within its folds, I'm transformed into another Elizabeth and feel pretty, very pretty. Because I shop so much, I'm hundreds of pretty Elizabeths, like flowers in a meadow. By being hundreds of Elizabeths, I can hide the child, the Little Bits, who once was me.

Little Bits is terrified. She's terrified because she, too, is remembering what Mommy and Daddy did to her. She's so terrified she feels littler than little, an itty, bitty ditty. Now that the remembering is getting done in the blood, I need to feel pretty, very pretty, to be hundreds of Elizabeths, not that terrified Little Bits, who's an itty, bitty ditty. I need to save her if I'm going to save me in order to save Ryan, so I hide her, disguise her.

In the dressing room, I glance in the mirror, at a pretty me, then wince because I also see the hurt Little Bits I was, who's hurt even more by the remembering. I step out of the throne room, go over to the jewelry case, scan it with the eyes of a murderer in a gun shop.

I tap the glass, say, "This, I want this." The woman who assists me enslaves me--my wrists are handcuffed with bracelets, my neck noosed by orange Moroccan beads. I whip out my credit card, slap it on the counter, like a gambler, or my great grandfather, Racehorse Charlie. If I can't race like a thoroughbred, I'll at least dress like one.

Outside, autumn drawls on. Red leaves are blown up as I drive home. I look at them with joy because all we are rivals this--red leaves blown up--like fire, like breath.

Before I go into my little house, shopping bag in tow, I see the last blue dragonflies. Their glinting wings never moan, not even when they dip, like oars in water deep enough to drown them. It's enough for them to rise and draw together like a bow. It's enough to watch them, to believe I'm the first woman to have seen anything, to love this moment: so brief and blue, uproarious. It's enough to know all of us depend on this--the end of summer, its shy light, the last dragonflies, bright as pansies, and the dazzle that delivers us, like a wild guess, from one day to the next.

Yet, as I enter the house, I'm hit by the madness. Reeling, careening, terror replaces wonder. My shopping bag goes flying. In it are the costly clothes bought just yesterday, including a belt not unlike the one Dad used to *snap, snap,* in my doorway at night.

I heard that belt go *snap* because I begged for a goodnight kiss. Now the belt goes *snap* while Dad hisses, *Shut up or you'll get this.* Suddenly, he's in my house, breathing everywhere. He's breathing, as if snorting the very electricity I run on and his cold, mulberry hands, smell like parsnips, as he creeps on me.

Mom gets in here, too. I, Little Bits, am terrified she'll whack me, again, with the bat. Her visage is leaden, like the lead pencil I grab to write with, scrawling big letters on the page. I'm ducking my head, screaming.

I'm eating my screams as I grab the pencil. Shaking, I do what I've never done before, write during the madness, write to get out of it, but Mom and Dad are on me.

"Stop it!" I scream, but they're attacking, full throttle, buzzing like fever bees, like demons, teeth-baring gods. I grope for my meds. Where are they? Somehow I find them, down them to drown out Mom and Dad, who are yelling at me because I've bought costly clothes to feel pretty, to hide the Little Bits that's me. They yell because I'm pretty, very pretty and Mom has no pity because I'm prettier than she, which is why Father wants me, not her, even though I'm an itty, bitty ditty.

Pause, pause, the meds start to kick in. My hand still shakes as I write big, big words, but the throttling, the buzzing stops and Mom and Dad recede, leaving me, a bunch of little bits, behind. As the meds kick in, I try to decipher the scrambled words, scrawled in big, big letters, on the page. I read my blocky letters--it's a show tune, loony tune, *I feel pretty, very pretty and witty and bright and I pity any girl who isn't me tonight.*

While reading this loony tune, I begin to hear the birds outside my windows pickaninny the lawn. I hear how the air is truffled with song. I also hear music in a distant room. In that room, the radio is on. It's loud enough to drown out the cries of the Little Bits I once was, of a pretty me, who isn't an itty, bitty ditty, but becoming my big, Kirschnerized being.

Because I'm becoming Kirschnerized, I know the remembering, which gets done in the blood, will have an end. When this happens, I'll be saner than I've ever been. Being sane will make me beautiful, so much so, a pretty me will no longer need to shop.

Shaky, but stabilized, I go outside. Here, I'm immersed in birdsong while I spy a white spider among the rugosas. She lifts her legs, moves her small, ghostly body across each flower, as moonlight does in my house. She is a snowflake, vanishing. Her quick fall from the bright sky matters. Her web is a beautiful hope easily undone, a fabric transient as tears. Even so, she lays it all upon these heady flowers which for her are the world: flushed, falling, gorgeous, mine.

V.
PING, PING, PING

In time, over time and through time, I continue to cross three bridges and states to see Ryan. In time, autumn gives birth to winter, cold as a cocktail. When that winter surrenders to spring, it's as though the gods have been appeased with gifts, not only from the dead, but my dead.

One such spring day finds me talking on the phone with my old friend, Scott, who's a builder. We're talking about rehabilitating my little house, which I'm now in the process of buying.

Scott's voice sounds as if it's jangling keys. His voice jangles as he goes over the inspection. "Elizabeth," he proceeds, "are you sure you know what you're doing? This camp is in rough shape."

"Yes, Scott," I say, as a waft of confidence fills me. "It's the spot. I really love the spot."

"That may be true, but there's a massive amount of work to be done on this place," he says, convinced I'm about to make a huge, grim error.

I'm staring hard at the water, watching panes of it shift like teutonic plates. "It's the spot," I murmur, my voice shakier now, "Can you at least come over and give me a bid?"

"Okay, okay, I'll come over tomorrow. I just don't want to see you make a big mistake."

"I know," I answer, "thank you."

He does come the next day. Tufts of green are roiling out of the gardens I dragged here. Silly birdsong plaits a low sky, heavy with clouds big as Gundalows. The azaleas pip: *good cheer, good cheer, to all who come near.* I put on a pot of coffee. Scott and I always have coffee when we get together.

He comes down the driveway on his Harley. I expected him to show up in his truck, so the Harley jars me. It sweeps me through trundling time until I'm on the rear of that bike one late October day, years before. Scott and I are in love. The day is unusually balmy. We've just dropped off his four year old boy with the boy's mother where his other child, a baby, is having a bath in the kitchen sink, paddling tiny hands in murky water. The movements in the water look like snow squalls. A squall, brisk, yet enduring, also stirs between Scott and his ex-wife. I find him beautiful: a burn scar, delicate as fossilized leaves, is ironed onto his forehead. Looking at him is like glancing into a delicately broken mirror: it is the delicacy that makes him moving. It still does.

On this particular morning, it's brisk and sugary outside. I'm washing dishes in my party-light strung kitchen when Scott comes down the driveway, dismounts his bike, knocks lightly on my kitchen door.

When I open it, I'm swept through trundling time again, yet not to years before, but six months earlier when, on another brisk morning, a sheriff stood in this same doorway in a wide swath of light. As I dried my hands on my apron, I stared at his hungover belly, cinched by a belt whose buckle gleamed like a brass knuckle. I was confused, frightened. Why was the sheriff at my house?

"Are you Elizabeth Kirschner?" he asked in a cold, formal manner. Suddenly, it felt like the whole neighborhood had been evacuated. Even the birds, those messengers of the divine, had vanished.

"Yes, what's wrong? What have I done?" I asked. My fear escalated. The sheriff blocked my doorway, his hand on his pistol holder. Was he trigger happy?

"Mrs. Kirschner," he announced, "I'm here to serve you your divorce papers."

"You're what?" I asked. "No, you must be wrong. My husband and I are mediating with our financial advisor."

The sheriff scratched his red, beefy nose, "Sorry, lady, but these are your divorce papers."

I wanted to tell him how our financial manager, Paulette, had drawn up a Vanilla Ice Cream plan with which to mediate, a plan she hoped would be sweet enough for Donald to swallow, but I shut up. The sheriff was looking impatient.

"Lady," he said, "just sign here."

The sheriff held out the divorce papers at arm's length, like a desperado. I took them, signed them. When I handed the papers back, he grabbed them, turned, got in his cop car and drove back down the driveway, sputtering gravel behind him.

The gravel sputtered in me, too. I stood in the kitchen doorway, wanting to shoot the sheriff. I wanted to shoot him as I watched the swath of light evaporate. Each particle pinged as it vanished--*ping,* went the light, *ping, ping, ping.*

As the light went, *ping,* I realized, *ping, ping,* that it had been exactly six months since our separation. I realized, *ping,* that Donald had waited exactly six months, *ping,* for me gain residency in the state of Maine. He waited, *ping,* so he could file against me in Maine, *ping,* because the divorce laws here are far less favorable to women than in Massachusetts, where the entire marriage had taken place. Donald waited until Paulette was out of the country and couldn't be reached. So much for her Vanilla Ice Cream plan, *ping, ping, ping.*

Now it's Scott who's getting off his bike, the one which kickstarted my memory. Now it's he, not the sheriff, who's standing in my kitchen door with all that silly birdsong yammering in the yard behind him. He smiles. Older, yes, but still beautiful with that delicate burn scar, like fossilized leaves, on his forehead. He walks right into my arms, gives me a hug.

"Elizabeth," he says, to which I simply answer, "Scott." There's a safety in just saying each other's names, as the years from before and now, this one, burst like bubbles until a freshness is restored to us. Soon, we're in the old living room on the cheap sofa drinking cheap coffee. Soon, we're walking through the house while Scott measures, asks questions.

"None of it's level," he mutters, "and there's a lot of mold, mildew, dry rot."

I'm not exactly level either, am also full of mold, mildew and dry rot so this doesn't phase me.

He looks into the tiny, downstairs bath. It has a telephone booth-sized shower whose back wall is my wailing wall because whenever

I come home from seeing Ryan, I take a shower, wail with the grief I feel over leaving him behind.

Scott asks, "Duct tape for a crack in the shower stall floor?"

"Duct tape fixes everything," I reply, vaguely wondering if I should duct tape my heart because it's leaky, too.

Scott cocks his head, bird-like, "The toilet," he begins.

I also cock my head, "I suppose it's listing a bit leeward."

"A bit?" he replies. Little do we know that the toilet is listing because the floor is rotted from a leak in the water heater situated in the adjacent furnace room. Little do we know that by rehabilitating my house, nail by nail, board by board, we'll also be rehabilitating me.

We go up to the loft where the water stains still look like strange amoebas. "This will have to be taken down to the studs." Scott says, but his brow is no longer creased. He seems to understand why I'm buying my Sea Cabin, that it is the spot, is the water beyond the old windows moving, like melted prisms, and the low clouds, which are suddenly pregnant with dreams, possibility.

He works out a bid. I don't even bother to get another one. Only Scott and I can rehabilitate this house and only Scott and I will.

VI.
BUT LEAP I DO

That same spring, a full year after the separation, singular songs are sleeping inside turgid buds while I stare out my study windows. There the clouds beak the sun and the water steals over me, like chain mail. I am alone, or should I say, alone with the dog and the cat, the day after the preliminary hearing for the divorce, a hearing which quickly deteriorated into something far less expected. My friend, Cleone, had driven me down to Boston to ensure that I would arrive at the courthouse psychically intact.

Inside the courtroom, my lawyer presented her plea before the Judge for a fair and equal distribution of the marriage holdings. Formidable, yes, but we had taken all rights to any portion of Donald's substantial inheritance from his father's estate off the table, as well as our beloved cottage in the Berkshires. My share of the 15 Debussy Circle house had already been distributed in order for me to buy and rehabilitate my Sea Cabin.

After my lawyer's elegant speech, Donald's lawyer, a former Baptist minister with an imposing stature, presented himself before the Judge. He started to rant, loudly, about my shopping. Shocked, I listened while this lawyer systematically assassinated my character due to my shopping. In preparation, this lawyer had seized my credit card statements. Figures from those statements punctuated the air, like the battery march of staccatos. Each of those staccatos hit me, hard.

The judge ordered Donald's lawyer to stop--again, again--but on he ranted, his voice so loud, it boomed. My lawyer tried to steady me by keeping her hand on my thigh, but as each staccato hit, my shaky stability shook some more. The Judge intervened, again, but Donald's lawyer wasn't about to desist.

When the next staccato hit, I felt whacked upside the head by Mother's bat. I screamed. The Judge's mallet pounded, repeatedly, until the full courtroom grew deathly still, except for my screams.

After being hauled out by guards, Cleone held me by my shoulders, told me to breathe and breathe I did. Because my brain was overmastered, calibrated even, to the pitch of my screams, I downed my meds. A nurse appeared, made it clear that I was not only going to be hauled out of the courtroom, but into the psych ward.

"No," I insisted, "I won't go," then added, "I need to go home." Cleone assured the nurse I'd be fine as she was driving me and would stay with me the night if need be. Somehow we got out of the courthouse, but not without Donald's lawyer glaring at me. When he asked Cleone who she was, she retorted, "None of your business," then quipped, "as far as I know shopping isn't a crime." Home we went in fog thick as oil paint.

It's the next day. As I stare out my study windows where clouds beak the sun and the waters continue to steal over me, I'm pondering the aggressive drive behind my character assassination, the divorce itself, and Donald. I'm seeing how his aggression is a sustained, systematic attempt to assuage his raging emptiness, an emptiness, I, too feel and glut, momentarily, by shopping. Such emptiness comes from his childhood and mine, the marriage itself, an emptiness I'll systematically heal, but he may not.

Is the emptiness that's driving Donald caused by my side of the marriage bed being brazenly empty, except for the Mother Shrine? Doesn't he believe I abandoned him and, in doing so, left him to care for our son? Isn't this chilling belief the one that threatens to annihilate him? Or is it his own cold, formal childhood?

I ponder this until, *boom,* I go crazy. *Boom,* I go crazy, but it's not great to be crazy or nuts like me. *Boom,* it's not great to be crazy or nuts like me, nor is it silly and foolish, yet *boom, boom,* I am.

While crazy and nuts, I think Donald is zipping me into a body bag. He's zipping me into a body bag to stuff me in the deep freeze, but how the hell did he get into my house? Where did he get the body bag? Worse, *why* is he also driving nails into the back of my head? The pain sears, my screams sear. Where are my meds?

After groping and groping, I find them. I remember to down them. After downing my meds, I start to come back. As I come back, I remember what time is and realize it's time to sob. Because it's time to sob, I sob very hard. I sob in order to wretch out the pain that's behind, not just my raging emptiness, but the madness itself. As I wretch out pain, my eyes close tight and, like a tiny astronaut, I'm untethered from the Mother ship.

Untethered, I'm totally alone. I wonder if the neighborhood has been evacuated, along with the birds, those messengers of the divine. Have I--*boom*--scared my neighbors, the gulls, and the self I call myself away because I, *boom,* went crazy again? If so, why wasn't I able to scare off Donald? If I'm unable to scare him off, how could I have ever scared Mother and Father away? Do I still need to don my skeleton costume to spook them all?

With difficulty, I get up and go into the kitchen. Because the party lights are on, I decide it's party time. I pour a glass of red wine, sip it. I also take a sleep med. I sip some more wine, take another med because I long to go off to a dreamland full of dancing fairies.

I go sit in my reading chair, pull Larka into my lap, pat her head, whisper, "Good girl." More wine, another med, more wine, yet another med. The clouds move like slow swans across the vernal sky. I hold my dog tight. I pet her head, whisper, "Good girl," again. If I wait long enough, will the big dipper come to scoop us up?

I'm getting very sleepy waiting for the big dipper to scoop us up. Sleepily, I write to Donald, my brothers, a few others: "I'm sipping wine, taking meds and going to dreamland, *bye-bye, bye-bye.*"

I'm pretty much all the way there, when suddenly, everything shatters. The air turns into glass splinters. Fists pound on my door, the windows in my study. The dog leaps from my lap, barks frenetically. The door breaks open, intruders clamor into my house. Hordes of EMTs and police close in on me, demand to know how many meds, how much wine. I swat them away like pesky flies, drawl answers, am a Southern belle,

"Hush little darlings, hush, hush."

I want to sing a lullaby, *hush, hush,* to my little darlings, but before I can I'm strapped onto a stretcher, ushered out of the house while

I whisper in a flirty voice, "O my darlings, take care of my dog and cat, you hear?"

Into the ambulance I go, my blood pressure taken, my veins too buried for the IV. Vague, disembodied voices speak kindly, so unlike the ones that shouted at me in ambulance after ambulance during the seizure years down in Boston. There the EMTs told jokes, even laughed while my strapped-down body contorted, jerked.

These EMTs are my dream escorts. Even so, the same questions are asked: how much wine, how many meds? By now, I'm too far gone to either swat at them, or drawl.

Once in the ER, off come my clothes, on goes the Jolly Green Giant johnny, the heart monitor, the IV finally started. Everything is surreal, except for the fairies dancing around my bed in sneakers.

Vaguely I wonder why they're wearing sneakers, not ballet slippers, but before this question gets answered, a doctor enters the ER, says, "You need to tell me how much wine you drank and how many meds you took."

"Hush," I reply, "just put your name on my dance card."

"Excuse me?" the doctor replies.

"Why, darling, can't you see I've all these lovely fairies to dance with before you?" I pause. Am I slurring my words? "Don't you worry, I have all the time in the world because I want to dance, dance, dance all night."

Worried, the doctor, pauses, then lifts a beaker to my lips. "Drink this," he quietly orders.

"Sorry, darling," I answer, definitely slurring my words, "I can't take communion because I haven't been to confession in years."

"Please," the doctor pleads, even more quietly, "you need to drink this. It's liquid charcoal and the medications, which haven't yet been absorbed into your blood, will bond to it, be flushed away."

Although he sounds like my biologist husband, he doesn't criticize me for slurring my words, so I slug down the brew, which tastes like Mom's poisonous communion. Before I can spit it out, I lose consciousness.

Hours, days, centuries later, I wake up. A nurse hovers over me, gently says, "Honey, you're in the ICU."

This vaguely registers. I look at her face, which bobs, a gushy balloon, near the ceiling. Her voice wafts in and out of me as she goes on, "We're monitoring you very closely. I'm sorry to say, but the medication you overdosed on could've affected your heart conductors."

This, too, vaguely registers. I want to tell her I didn't overdose. I want to say I was just trying to get to dreamland, but am too nauseous to do so. I'm overwhelmingly nauseous, so much so, my tummy is doing perfect belly flops.

I reel in my nausea, my tummy continuing to belly flop as I float in and out of drugged sleep. I float in and out all night long. At times, I almost gag on vomit as it rises from the sick pit of my tummy.

As dawn arrives, it achingly dawns on me that I've poisoned myself with my own, not Mom's, poisonous communion. The body I've betrayed is sick from that betrayal. The sickness stays while another dawning comes: the remembrance of messages I'd sent to Donald, my brothers, a few others: *bye-bye, bye-bye*. Surely, I've scared them out of their wits just because I was out of mine.

I tell this to the nurse. Moments later, a laptop miraculously appears. Shakily, with one finger, like a walking stick for the blind, I tap on the keys: *ok, in the icu, so sorry*. With the other hand, I clutch my belly, which continues to surge with my poisonous communion while another dawning occurs: *Ryan*.

Before I can think about Ryan, the doctor comes in. He asks more questions, but this time I answer them like the obedient child I once was. He notes how much wine I drink daily, mumbles something about substance abuse.

"You don't understand," I counter, "I'm the one who was abused."

The doctor simply nods his head, makes a note in his chart. "I'm giving you medical clearance to have you released from the ICU."

"Where will I go?" I ask.

"The psych ward," he replies, as though it's Alice's Wonderland.

My sick stomach gets sicker. The psych ward. No, not again. Not the lock-up.

"This is protocol," the doctor states, "a group called Crisis Intervention will determine the final outcome. In the state Maine, there's a Blue Paper that can involuntarily put you in the Unit."

The Blue Paper, that document of the damned. What I want to say is, I *don't want the Blue Paper*. I want to say, *Can't I be dismissed?* and, *Can you please excuse me from detention?* Certainly being served the Blue Paper is worse than being served divorce papers by the Sheriff I wanted to shoot.

The doctor leaves. Fragile, ill, barely there, I crumple into bed, sink into queasy sleep. Upon awakening, the man from Crisis Intervention is hovering at the foot of my bed. I bolt upright, get ready to be steady, upbeat in order to avoid The Blue Paper.

He's straight with me. "That was an awful lot of wine and medication you took. We need to keep you safe."

I'm straight with him. "I know, I know, I drank way too much wine, took too many meds, but I'm going through a difficult divorce and my childhood was even worse."

"I get it," he says, "but we can keep you safe in the Unit. We need to do that."

"I promise it won't happen again."

"Listen," he insists, "we must keep you safe."

I'm sure he has the upper hand and I'll be toeing the red line before I know it. "I can go to a friend's house," I suggest, "I'll be safe with a friend."

"Who?" he asks.

I reel off a list of names, as if from my dance card: *Lillie, Mimi, Kelsey, Marguerite, Linda.* I'm hoping that one, like a catchy tune, will appeal. *Kelsey.* We land on *Kelsey.*

Hours later, Kelsey appears, not exactly like a fairy, but close enough. She helps me get dressed. She steadies a very unsteady me, as though she's a helping verb and the helping verb I need is the word *be.* I need to learn how to *be* all over again. More so, I need to *be* for Ryan.

We walk out of the hospital, drive off in her little blue car. We stop for Ginger ale and crackers for my tummy.

Kelsey takes me to her yellow house where she nurses me. Minutes, hours, centuries later, we take a walk on Sea Point beach. At the beach, I come to understand that the divorce will get settled. When the divorce gets settled, we'll arrive at Paulette's Vanilla Ice Cream plan, only after spending hundreds of thousands of dollars on legal fees. When the divorce gets settled, the judge's mallet will come down, as if to decree that I'm solidly sane, which I will be because I'm no longer be married to a staler, paler version of my father.

At the beach, spring in its redundancy, dons its green frock to release the ecstasy of the secret smells beneath the wind's neat pleats. As I inhale the ecstasy of these smells, Ryan's name becomes my one-word prayer, one-word poem and I vow to never let go of my hold on terra firma again. As I exhale, a butterfly, light as his spirit, flies through the velvet hips of spring.

As that butterfly flies through spring's velvet hips, fish, glittery as lures, leap out of cresting waves. My plunge, into depths too deep to fathom, may have preceded my leap, but leap I do, with glittery fish. As I leap out of the depths, I'm a muscle of infinite reception and, for a moment long enough to last a lifetime, I'm splendidly spilling, splendidly alive.

Two:

NEW YORK

1955-1963

"Gazebo through a Window"

VII. LITTLE BITS FALLS FROM GRACE

I may have once been a respectable baby, but now that I can get dressed all by myself, I'm a big girl. I know I was a respectable baby, who grew from a magic bean planted in Mommy's belly. I grew in Mommy's belly, until I was born in a hospital, just like any other respectable baby. Mommy says I was a little firecracker who went off too soon--it was noontime on the 3rd of July. It was also ninety degrees in the shade.

I don't remember being born, but I suppose most respectable babies don't. It seems wrong that we don't remember the moment of our births, especially since, as far as I know, we only get born once. It's a shame that we don't remember our births and plainly, a needless oversight in God's divine Plan.

Oversight or not, I somehow or other most assuredly got myself born. I came thundering down Mommy's birth canal, headfirst. I don't know why I came thundering down Mommy's birth canal headfirst because it seems to me that coming into the world feet first would have been a more sensible choice. Maybe I would have landed, like a cat, on those very feet. Had I come into the world feet first, God may have made an exception in his needlessly flawed divine Plan, in order to grant me nine lives.

I came into the world with a big *whoosh* sound and if I didn't exactly thunder, well then, my soul did. Or it clashed like cymbals after a big roll on the timpani. Clearly some loud, glorious sound, some celestial orchestration accompanied the moment of my birth right there in Glen Head Hospital in Glen Cove, NY, but Mommy didn't hear it because she was knocked out cold.

Clash-Clash, Rat-a-tat-tat, and bingo! I got myself born. Once Mommy came round, she instantly saw me for the blessed, adorable babe I was. How could she not with the dove-like cooing I did while she held me, adoringly, in her arms? All that cooing made her see the holiness in me, or maybe it was the angel wings that were rooted in the wee ears of my shoulder blades. Either way, my blessedness is how I account for her giving me one of the holiest names around, Elizabeth Mary.

Names don't get any holier. Not only was I named after Mother Mary, but also after her sister. Besides, Elizabeth Mary makes up two falling dactyls, so it's perfectly poetic. Once Mommy deemed her blessed babe Elizabeth Mary, I revved up my cooing. It must have sounded like one-hundred thousand doves cooing right there in the maternity ward at Glen Head Hospital. I bet the nurses are still talking about the day when that blessed babe, Elizabeth Mary, most assuredly got herself born with her cooing henceforth and ever flowing.

As I cooed, my soul was up-fluttering on my lips. How could Mommy not see that my up-fluttering soul was the embodiment of my state of grace? Can you imagine giving birth to a baby who was also in a state of grace? No wonder she quit having children after me. I was her best magic bean yet.

Well, being Mommy's best magic bean didn't last long. I sure hope she appreciated it while it did. Even the best beans can go to hell in a hand basket. I started to fall from my state of grace the day Mommy took me home from Glen Head Hospital.

Imagine Mommy carrying me, like the precious bundle I was, into the little brown house on Sherman Road. Imagine her unwrapping the bundle I was for my not-so-precious brothers and sister to adore. Imagine my not-so-precious brothers and sister clambering around Mommy as she unwrapped me, then waiting to hear some rapturous *oohs* and *ahs*.

No *oohs* and *ahs* came, not even when I cooed, or let my soul up-flutter on my lips. For a moment, my clambering, not-so-precious brothers and sister were dead silent. They were silent until Danny burst out, "She looks like a big, fat hamburger, just like a big, fat hamburger. Let's call her Little Bits."

"Little Bits, Little Bits," Danny, Gene and Marie all screamed, laughing, "She's just a big, fat hamburger. Let's call her Little Bits."

Little Bits it was. Therein began my fall from my state of grace and, cat-like or otherwise, it's pretty hard to land on your feet when you're going to hell in a hand basket. Therein ended my life as a respectable baby, let alone a blessed or adorable one, and my life as Little Bits, began. Little Bits indeed.

VIII.
LITTLE BITS TASTES THE COLD DELICIOUSNESS OF HER YUMMY, EDIBLE LIFE

I start to wake up. My head feels cradled by Grandma's goose-feather pillows as I turn to look at the evergreen light shawling from her high transom windows. I breathe in the balsam-scented air while recalling my dancing dream of fairies, the one which came to me during a night long as a bolt of silk.

Grandma, whose body is a warm berm, draws me close. Her heat is that of cream in coffee, or custard sprinkled with nutmeg. For a moment, my life is yummy, edible.

"How's my Guardian Angel?" she asks, alert and drowsy at the same time. It's her drowsiness that lures me, like a snore so quiet, it makes me purr.

"I'm yummy, Grammy," I say as I noodle my way into her. "Did you sleep well?"

"Yes, Little Bits," she replies, "you barely stirred all night as you were cocooned right next to me."

"I had dancing dreams," I say while plying my fingers in the puckers of Grandma's satin, pewter-colored quilt. The buttons feel like the ones on little dolls' dresses, ivory buttons, or even mother-of-pearl.

"Guess what?" asks Grandma. As she asks this, I look into her blue eyes, which look distilled by the scent of blue rain caught in her silver hair.

"What?" I ask, while stifling a long, spidery yawn.

"I need help making the pancakes. Do you think my Guardian Angel can help me?"

"Please," I pip, in tandem with the bird notes trilling through the transom windows, notes bright as silvery coins. "Please let me be your helper."

"Of course you can, but even Guardian Angels need to get dressed before they can be little helpers."

"I can get dressed all by myself," I announce, as I get out of Grandma's bed. In evergreen light, I tug off my baseball pajamas, pull on my clean girl undies, undershirt and white turtleneck, step into my baby blue corduroy overalls and fasten the two heart buttons on the straps. They're slippery, but I'm determined to get them done all by myself.

Grandma pats my head, "Splendid," she says. I feel my heart beam and the beam tickles me pink. I didn't know hearts could beam, let alone tickle oneself pink.

I lift Grandma's brush off her vanity to run it through my short, mousy-brown hair. The bristles are soft as antennae and smell like talcing powder. Little forget-me-nots are sprinkled on the ivory handle.

"Who's your favorite Guardian Angel?" I ask while toying with one of the heart buttons on my overalls.

"Little Bits," Grandma starts, "you're my only Guardian Angel. That makes you my favorite, doesn't it? Now let's go find my little helper apron."

Into the kitchen we go, hand-in-hand, like two old sweethearts. Grandma pulls out a small, starched apron from the drawer next to the iron sink. When she puts it on me, the flounces flare out like cake frosting.

Out comes Grandma's green bowl, which she sets down on the floral, enamel table. In goes flour, baking powder and milk from the ice box. In goes charity, moonlight and disaster, plus red, red roses, simple as a stitch, from all the gardens she's ever made. In goes eggs, holy water and novenas, for this is Grandma's green bowl, deep enough for trees to take hold, for pennies from heaven to fall into, for all we never dreamed of to be shared and broken, broken and shared.

"Roll up your sleeves now," Grandma says, "and mix it all up."

I slip in my hands, work the dough to mix up sugar-snow and feeder roots, lace and orange rinds. Maybe the lumps in the dough are Grandma's red, red roses from her gardens, big as storybooks. Maybe the pennies from heaven are manna.

"Grammy, are these manna pancakes?" I ask.

"Of course, they are, sweetie," she answers while smiling with her insider's radiance.

"This is much better than making mud pies," I exclaim, as I pat my hands together and *Pouf!* the kitchen is filled with floury clouds. Everything seems otherworldly--the window curtains above the sink are bright party favors, the ice box might as well be filled with angel hair and the light is just plain celestial. I whisper, "Do you think we've died and gone to heaven?"

Grandma smiles. Her lilac-colored cheeks smell like the tender undersides of spring leaves. "Guardian Angels always have one foot in heaven and one on earth," she says, carefully.

"Does that mean me?" I ask, shy as a bride.

"Yes," she answers so solemnly it sounds like a prayer.

"Amen," I respond, then pause before asking, "Griddle time?"

"Griddle time."

Grandma helps me flip one or two manna pancakes and lets me shake confectioners' sugar all over the batch.

We sit down to eat. I keep my apron on because it's so pretty. "Do you think they serve manna pancakes in greasy spoons?" I ask. Somehow this feels like a serious religious question.

"Yes," Grandma answers, then continues, "just think of Holy Communion as mini-manna pancakes."

"But I'm too little for Holy Communion," I say.

"Ah, but even Little Bits will be big enough for that someday."

"Praise the Lord," I say in my biggest, big girl voice, then dig into my manna pancakes. Grandma smiles as I eat, not just bite after bite of manna pancakes, but my yummy life as well--at least it's so when I'm with her, which is good enough.

After manna pancakes, Grandma sweeps me off the kitchen chair and presses me tight to her breasts, which are yeasty and redolent as baby birds. She carries me into the parlor and turns on the Wurlitzer. It whines like an old saint in the junkyard. We waltz through the rooms in her small walk-up to the music of Lawrence Welk and Li Po.

We waltz to the music of Schumann and Wallace Stevens, Keats and Rogers and Hammerstein. We waltz, feel eternal and, for a small eternity, we are.

* * *

At home I'm just Little Bits, not Grandma's Guardian Angel. Sometimes I put Grandma's little helper apron on over my blue overalls, so I can at least pretend to be her Guardian Angel. I'm hoping that if I pretend to be her Guardian Angel long enough, the state of grace I fell from after my birth, will be reinstated.

One afternoon, I put Grandma's apron on over my overalls to see if Mommy will let me help make the meatloaf. I want to mix the meat up just like I did the pancake dough.

I'm about to ask Mother if I can be her helper when I hear the ice cream man come ding-dinging down Sherman Road.

When I hear the ice cream man come dinging down Sherman Road, I'm standing on the black-and-white tiled chessboard floor, staring at Mommy's tight, bowling pin calves sheathed in nylons beneath a cocktail dress and frilly apron. Pots and pans rattle as if in a big brass band. Outside, my noisy brothers and sister play on the Slip and Slide, which is bright as the oceanic sky above them. They go down it like a chute in Chutes and Ladders, laughing, laughing all the way.

When Mother says, "I'm watching you with eyes in the back of my head," I look for them. Are they insect eyes: a cockroach's, or the itsy-bitsy spider in her spider-well?

As the ice cream truck comes ding-dinging its way down Sherman Road, my brothers and sister run into the kitchen, grab nickels from Mother's coffee can money, dash back out the door to buy ice cream cones.

She warns me again, "Look out, Little Bits, I'm watching you with the eyes in the back of my head," then rattles more pots and pans.

I grab a nickel while looking for these eyes. I look hard, but instead of finding insect eyes, I see demons attacking her. These demons have red-and-black reptilian wings, attack her like a horde of fever bees. Or are they pit-bullish, teeth-baring gods? Do I hear screams buzzing in her, buzzing out of her, blitzing the light out of her, out of me, feverishly, as her nerves, my nerves, are zapped by sword-flashing lightning?

Buzzed and blitzed, Mommy whips a baseball bat out from the broom closet, slams it into the back of my head. I hear the thwack, then fall like a scarecrow in a heap of broken straw. Pain, like black ice fills me. Light cries its way out of my body, bleeds all over the chessboard floor where I have fallen, a poor pawn, at three or four.

When Mommy hits the back of my head with the sweet spot of the bat, I roll--a stunned fish--while she plunges knives into dirty dishwater to finish killing the demons. My eyes slam shut, like garage doors.

Behind these doors, I inhale fumes, deathly and phosphorescent. Moths salve me with the dust on their wings--I become a wizened child with grey hair, bones full of hot wires. I descend into the demons, into the gods, am content, but can't know that I'm descending beyond the demons and the gods because I'm going into the below-land of my being where to feel is an afterthought better not thought at all, so I don't feel, nor do I remember what has just happened. Rather my memory sleeps, like Sleeping Beauty.

What I do feel when I come back is an ice-capped, black isolation in my head as I stare at my brothers and sister while they suck ice cream out of the pointy ends of their ice cream cones, laughing, laughing all the way. They don't know that Mother was just attacked, nor do they know she whacked me with the bat. They don't know, never will, nor do they know that the Little Bits she whacked is now a gray-haired, wizened child with bones full of hot wires.

My brothers and sister clamor, "Little Bits, Little Bits, have a lick of ice cream," as though I still existed. When I do lick some of that cold deliciousness, it tastes like the cold, black-capped isolation in my head. It also tastes like love because only love can follow the stricken thereafter and love is what my yummy, edible life tastes like.

IX.
LITTLE BITS DREAMS OF GRANDMA'S RED, RED ROSES

Because love follows the stricken thereafter, no one can see that I, Little Bits, am a gray-haired child with bones full of hot wires. Nor does anyone see my gnarly wisdom, or my visions of clouds turning into wet, blue swans. They don't see the cold, coke-bottle thickness in my head. Little Bits remains Little Bits.

When winter comes I go out after big storms to make snow angels. I flap my arms and legs fast, like windshield wipers, to make the wings and gown. It's deliriously cold, so much so, the black-capped ache in my head feels majestic, like a summit banked in clouds--my Eden iced over. My fingers and toes get cold, are full of fever bees, which carry me into dreams where flames encircle my body, but do not ignite me. I want to be carried into these fever dreams, into the incendiary, seismic buzz of existence: I flap my arms and legs even harder, willing my soul to take *flight, flight.*

While waiting for my soul to take *flight,* I notice that it's not just cold, it's also quiet. This quiet tastes like vanilla spiced with an after-bite of cardamon. I didn't know the quiet could taste like spiced vanilla, but I long for that taste to last a lifetime. While longing for that taste to last, the quiet goes, *whir, whir,* inside my body.

The *whir* inside my body is the sound butterflies make when in migration. I know this because I've seen them migrate. Late last summer, Mommy took us all to the beach.

There I filled green coke bottles, thick as my ice-capped head, with itty-bitty whelks. These itty-bitty whelks had itty-bitty holes drilled in them by a prehistoric sea creature.

This sea creature sucked their insides out. I knew what those itty bitty whelks felt like when having their insides sucked out because that's what Daddy does when he creeps on me. Does that make him a prehistoric creature, too?

At the beach, I heard a *whir,* looked up. The sky was suddenly alit with hundreds upon thousands of monarchs, dazzling, like bright, orange bows. Even more suddenly, I was plunged into a fairyland.

This fairyland was like the one I had dreamed of, but now I was wide awake and it wasn't just for me. Danny, Gene and Marie, even Mommy all gazed up at the hundreds upon thousands of monarch butterflies. They went *whir* in an ever-shifting crazy quilt, a moving, flitting rag tail collage while we gazers danced in a trance.

Even I, Little Bits, knew the monarchs would vanish soon. They would begin their long, perilous migration. We all did. Still, we longed to hoard these hordes of monarchs, to have them alight on us like tiny flashcards.

As the monarchs went *whir* I realized that they had little bits of precocious genius tucked into the tiny machines of their bodies. This was also tucked into the Little Bits that was me. I saw that these bits of precocious genius had boldness and power and magic in them. This meant that I had boldness and magic and power. It hit me like a power voltage.

Suddenly my bits of precocious genius were knocked on. It was contagious as laughter, widespread as wildfire, especially when the monarchs alighted upon me and my brothers and sister, even Mommy. The monarchs alighted, then bolted, often at the same time.

Now as the *whir* continues inside my body, I expect the sky to fill with thousands of butterflies. Instead, the sky is lofted with big, fat snowflakes. These snowflakes swoon down to ground, settle on my eyelashes and toes, like emissaries of the very angel I'm making. In my snowy wilderness, I, Little Bits, see that nine times out of ten, heaven is here. If heaven is here, then surely my bits of precocious genius are infused with the divine. Won't this sheer blessedness reinstate my own angel-ness? How could it be otherwise?

Little Bits, Little Bits, I hear in this snowy wilderness, *I'm coming to get you.* I freeze, stop flapping my arms and legs. *Little Bits, I'm coming to get you.*

It's Daddy. He's coming to creep on me. I want to run, but before I can get up out of my snow angel, he's on me. He pushes me in my angel, which is hard as cracked paraffin. His breath is clammy. It hits me, like an accident. He creeps and creeps, yanks down my snowsuit and overalls, does what he does to me.

As he creeps, does what he does, he's overshadowed by sadness, a sadness no one but I can see. This sadness is so old and cold, it causes his soul to go mad, inhumanly, the way my own mind will decades later. Inhuman, he does what he does, desecrating a me that isn't me, one who is, sadly, his Little Bits.

Inhuman, he seeds me while all the falling snow explodes into gunpowder. When the snow explodes into gunpowder, all of creation bangs, breaks, furiously expands as Father says, *you're no angel.*

When he says this, his own dark angel descends into a death so vast, it doesn't, can't, won't ever come back while mine bangs, breaks furiously into creation. Like this falling snow, my angel is a wild, white magnificence.

Still, breakage is the wildest danger--beastly, dreadful--and I'm just Little Bits, my me, my thou, which Daddy has turned into an *it* before trudging off, leaving me, an *it,* in the falling snow, which falls like sleep dust into the Sleeping Beauty I am, dreaming of Grandma's red, red roses.

X.
LITTLE BITS PICKS UP STICKS AFTER THE BIG STORM

Whatever Father seeded in me retreated into my own sleeping depths where it overwintered for decades. After overwintering, this dreadful seed ripped through me, wrung itself open, then wondrously blundered into a manic season of blossoming. This season happened in the unlikeliest of times, a time dawning only after Father's death, Mother's, the death of my marriage, a time beyond the erupting intrusion of my transfiguring madness and my need to be hundreds of Elizabeths, a time when I let time heal me and allowed my Savage Maker to enter my inmost thou, to enshrine me with the thou that's deepest in me, the thou Father almost did in, but couldn't because survivors are always stronger than their perpetrators.

Still, before that wretched seed was wrought to whammy me into this unlikely, but joyful season of blossoming in the long, succulent autumn I call my life, I, Little Bits, was impaired by wounds no one could see. I was impaired by the iced-over Eden in my head and my ripped-open insides, so I retreated--*deeply, deeply*--into the vast blue woods of my childhood. In these woods, my visions thundered like an onslaught of trumpets, like stars sparking in the heavens and the black anise that mars the wounds in trees with tarry pools.

I, Little Bits, dost remain in the vast, blue woods of my childhood from scantest dawn to decanted twilight, rare as the cherry womb of a lady-slipper. Here I scramble onto downed trunks whose roots span the girth of Catherine wheels, trunks whose spongy insides are stuffed with what seems like crimson-brown catkins. I wonder: does the catkin fairy nest in that puffy fluff? Does she dingle-dangle on twigs, or slinky-slink with sea-green inchworms?

I ponder this while holding onto a root system, my Catherine wheel, with my hands at the ten and the two. I feel this Catherine wheel give as the spongy insides of the tree trunk exhume a heady perfume, one that has aged in its oak barrel until the crimson-brown catkins smell like molasses-soaked hay.

As the odor of hay is exhumed from the insides of the tree trunk, the blue woods of my childhood become redolent with a sweetness that's absent elsewhere. Does this sweetness hatch from the insect eggs speckled, like dotted Swiss, on umbrella-shaped leaves? Does it emanate from the musky baleen titillating the undersides of mushrooms pricked like coral parasols into the mulched earth, or is it what's packed in the acorns I press to my ears to hear the ocean inside them, the very ocean I'll come to live by in the succulent autumn I call my life?

While I walk in this homemade brewery of sweetness, it sticks to my own spongy insides, until I, too, reek of molasses-soaked hay. Reeking, my insides turn into caviar as I poke at ugly bugs, which are mired in damp leaf mat. I feel sea-green inch worms slinky-slink in my mousy brown hair, can't help but hope a catkin fairy will nest there.

I enshrine tree stumps with skull caps made from emerald mosses, soft as lambswool. The mosses' blooms look like red eye stalks, or common pins. Can anyone hear these pins, which do not fall, but bloom in the deep, blue woods? How many angels dance on each and are they a higher rank of angels? Is my white, magnificent one in the highest ranks?

I hope so as I kneel before my enshrined tree stumps. Once Mother glued my hands together in prayer because I'd played with the ribbons of her Missal during Mass. This prompts me to pray,

"Holy Mary, don't let Mommy glue my hands together again. It's hard to sleep with them glued and it hurts, Amen."

I get up, walk some more in the brewery of the woods. My happiness quickens because my insides have turned into caviar. Reeking of hay, I leave a scent trail in woods that are a vast, verdant vestibule. Here, the trees are taller than steeples. I love to wrap my arms around them, as if they're Mother's legs. She, too, is a dark, twisted bitter root. Nothing can pull her from this earth, or so it seems, and in this alone, I am like her.

As I walk deeper into the woods, leaving a scent trail, I hear twigs start to snap, like wishbones. Wishes trill out of me, just in case they really are wishbones. "I wish my mind was as bright as a lighthouse," is the first one. "I wish these trees were totem poles for my soul to sleep in," is the second. Then I make a third, knowing that wishes can't come true if you don't make three by saying, "I wish my ears were magnets to music." Another twig *snap, snaps.*

Shy as a bride, I turn around, see Daddy wearing a hunter orange hat.

"Little Bits," he says, "I'll make your wishes come true."

"Really?" I ask.

"Follow me," he says quietly.

I do. He leads me to my Playhouse. I go in, ask, "Are we going to have a tea party? I love tea parties. We can pretend we're eating Grandma's ladyfingers."

"Yes," Father says. I sit down at my tea table. On it are Dixie cups full of violets I'd picked for Mommy, hid in the kitchen cupboards for her to find and when she didn't, I made a centerpiece out of them for my Playhouse. They're wilted, but still hold their Lenten color and are as soft as the insides of my dog's ear.

"Ladies lift their little fingers when they drink tea and eat ladyfingers," I say, "like this." When I lift my little finger and look up with my pretend teacup, Father has my Patty Play.

"This is what I'll do to you," he says, "if you don't comply." Because his soul's mad, he takes out his knife, c*ut, cuts,* into my Patty Play Pal's limbs. They fall like plastic socks.

"No," I say in my big girl voice, "I won't comply and you, Daddy, aren't allowed to hurt me." When I yell, "You aren't allowed to hurt me," a second time, his face goes dark. As his face grows dark, his angel blackens. In turn, my white magnificent one becomes frost fire.

As frost fire, I don't feel it when Father pushes me to the floor, lifts my turquoise top with the snowballs on it to *cut* angel wings into my shoulder blades. Instead, I flex the wings he's tooling into me in order to take *flight, flight.* Before I take *flight,* I let my frost fire glint, like a sneer on his blade. My frost fire not only glints like a sneer, it also sears him, coldly. Seared, he goes into a state of torpor as he backs out of my Playhouse.

In that torpor, he doesn't, can't, won't ever harm me again and this is when my soul takes *flight.* My soul takes *flight,* goes to dingle-dangle on the twigs and slinky-slink with inch worms. If I didn't take flight, I'd die.

Maybe I do die. I don't know. I don't know because when I start to come back, it's dark. It's dark and a sticky web maps my back. I'm lying on the floor of the Playhouse, am just Little Bits with a web mapping my back. I pull down my turquoise top with the white snowballs on it, tug on Dad's hunter orange hat, then go down to the lagoon at the bottom of the woods. Here I'll no longer remember what has happened, nor to whom or what I'll return.

At the lagoon, I wade through weeping willows which dowse the dark shore, like beaded curtains. I find a bag of bread and place soft hunks on the scummy water as though each piece were a boat of sorrow momentous to no one but my quiet and captive self. Swans, dense with the exhumed perfume the woods reek of, surge among loose lilies. Two braid their necks together in pear-colored moonlight. I wash the web off my back, listen to the sounds the lonely intuit and trust. I crouch in swamp grass, flightless, homeless, and full of peace, as swans, in their low white dresses, lift wings, heavy as dinner plates, to gain the cool ground about me.

In time, I return home, don my skeleton costume, go to bed. During the night, a storm ignites the skies. Spikes of sword-flashing lightning impale treetops until they let loose blazing fluorescent hair. I want the lightning to spike me, to martyr me in its fire, like those who sing while they burn, joyous in their deaths. When more lightning impales the treetops and I'm not martyred, I feel the bones in my skeleton costume ignite, like fire bones, or the bones of a house I'll someday wake by the sea.

These bones will burn me into rightful joy and they'll procreate me. I'll be procreated with the balm of chastened water, with blossoms, frivolous as laughter, and my own buttery succulence. I'll be procreated with the soft tissues of loss and a goodness far more lordly than gaunt. More lordly than gaunt, I drift off to sleep, dream of Grandma's red, red roses, falling simple as a stitch

Next morning, I get up, walk in my skeleton costume into the kitchen. There I stare at my cool, blue glass of milk, nibble on toast dusted with cinnamon and desire. I keep my head down, even if I'm more lordly than gaunt, I'm still penitential. Haven't I been sentenced by the condemned, by own parents, who harm me because they think I deserve to go to the hell they create? Aren't they the ones condemned to the hellishness of who they are?

When I glance up at the condemned, neither Father or Mother can lift up their eyes to me, their thine, their thou. Not only that, but they'll never be able to lift up their eyes to me, again, because of the unnameable shame they feel toward me, a shame so deep it cleaves them. Cleaved, they not only forget this shame, but why it's there. Cleaved, they need their shame to shame me and make it my caul.

"Little Bits," Dad starts, "go out into the yard to pick up the big sticks that came down in the storm. Everybody else can go play."

Cauled, I obey. I go out, pick up the storm-stricken sticks. The air is plush as the mosses I use to enshrine the tree stumps. Sunlight, energy shims between branches frocked in green as I bend to pick up sticks. There I notice a red salamander, sleek as a baby's finger, hiding in a cave of grass. I long to cup this salamander in my hands-it's eerily aglow, but don't wish to frighten it in grass long and streaked with silver: each blade holds the delicacy that lasts after frost after frost has been heaped upon it. This delicacy draws me, as my ears are drawn, like magnets, to the zithery music the blades make.

Dropping to my knees, I comb each strand to embellish this music with the weighty notes of cellos. I then gather twigs, small as matches. I gather them as if gathering a bouquet of bones. No one understands a child's mind, its fabled inventions, but years later, I'll carry these bone-twigs, small as matches, to build my own nest in a house by the sea. There, the birds will carry these bone-twigs away, one by one. When the birds carry them away, they do so to nest in in trees close to my Sea Cabin. In doing so, they carry away my caul, like a golden veil trailed over centuries.

Three:

ROCKFORD AND BEYOND

1963-1989

"Sea Shanty"

XI.
ANGEL FACE

When I'm eight years old, we move. The drama of this move, intentional or not, stops the violence Mom and Dad perpetrate upon me. We move from Glen Cove, New York to Rockford, Illinois, in the heart of the heart of the country, where the only sea is of cornfields. Here, their violence goes underground to burrow beneath the long, cold winters that come to scour our barren landscape. Here, the winds are more resolute than my will, yet this is where I, Little Bits, turn into the cornsilk concealed beneath tough husks. Still, I won't be able recognize this silkiness, or my toughness, until I enter the bright world to live by the sea.

My school days pass like blank flashcards, but Saturdays find me down in the basement, hiding behind the stairs. Decades later, when my mind goes inhumanly mad, like Dad's soul, hiding will become my forté--in closets, under the vanity, one day will even find me trying to squeeze into the dog's crate. I need to hide, in order to make sure Mom and Dad can't hurt the Little Bits that's me. I'll hide from them long after they both die their ghastly deaths, but at age eight, I hide by squeezing myself between the riser-like basement stairs. I can shimmy myself between the stairs because I'm thin as a ladder of scrimshaw bone. Here, I sit, cross-legged, like a primitive mud statue. I sit and stare through the slats between the stairs, as though they were Venetian blinds, while the odor of chalk and molt sweats from the basement walls.

Through the slats between the stairs, I watch my father at his workbench. His back is to me, like the priest's at High Mass. On Saturdays, Dad goes to his workbench. On Saturdays, I hide behind the basement stairs. Above the workbench, his tools are arranged on a peg board. In drawers that wordlessly slide in and out, nuts and bolts are organized, like Stein's tender buttons.

The drawers slide in and out while Father removes nuts and bolts, sets to work, as if at the high ministries of an anointed office. He sings as he works, in a voice turning the old screws of loneliness and loss into me. He shuffle-steps from side-to-side while he sings, *Angel Face, you've got the cutest little Angel Face.* In a voice turning screws, he sings the wrong words on purpose, *You've got the cutest little Angel Face,* then shuffle-steps some more.

He sings the wrong words to me. Even though I'm hiding behind the cellar stairs, he knows I'm there. He always does--maybe my soul makes opulent ripples from a pebble dropped into the mossy well of my inmost being. Or does my heartbeat give off sonic vibrations, as though wooed from a blue harmonica?

Dad sings the wrong words, *Angel Face, you've got the cutest little Angel Face*, as if courting the Little Bits he abhorrently violated. This sickens me--my tummy does perfect belly flops while sweat weeps from our molting basement walls. As my tummy sickens, my soul needs, must rise, until it hovers, star-wise and planetary in an airy aperture. The starry aperture marbles my soul with a meaning only I can intuit and trust, one which inflates, like a cloud bowled over with snow, *be unlike, be unfinished, be forever begun.*

Father keeps singing, *You've got the cutest little Angel face*, even though he once swore I was no angel. In spite of this, I feel my angelness inflate, *be unlike.* This fills me--wild, white, magnificent--until my soul swirls into the planetary aperture while the wings Dad carved into my shoulder blades start to twitch. They twitch, flex, the moment he spins away from the altar of his workbench and sings right out, "Angel face, I'm in heaven when in your embrace."

Father's words are sickening. I breathe. *I'm in heaven*--I breathe in his sickness, and the scent of chalk and molt, which flavors the vomit rising in the back of my throat. *I'm in heaven when in your embrace.* My tummy roils, belly flops. How can he not feel how sickening he is?

Pulled by an inaudible cue, Dad turns away. He turns back to his anointed office, to a world darkened by the darkest manly sense. I exhale. Out goes his sickness, smelling of chalk, but some of it remains, causing my mind to go mad, decades later.

Father is transfixed at his workbench. He could be repairing crucifixes, or cobbling the shoes of the angel I am. It doesn't matter because, in this moment, I'm drawn outward, like a flame drawn to the air that will consume it, to the shimmery ether at its tip where order and turbulence abound. Or am I a magnet pulling away from the underworld of the basement? Is this magnet being drawn toward the music I'm meant to perform on earth?

Drawn outward, I leave the basement, get out of the house. I get out, let the screen door bang behind me. A year or two passes as I enter the deep blue woods of my childhood, which migrated with me when we moved.

In these migrating woods, moods stew in me, heavy as liqueur. Under the generous awning of the evergreens, I taste the liqueur in my moody stew, hot as cinnamon, or pepper flakes. I wander the woods, as wandering is what I'm want to do--each path is a mineshaft that might hold the darkest jewels. Dreamily, I believe these jewels are edible, like caviar. I bend, load them into the pockets of my Scout uniform, then press an acorn to my ear to hear the ocean.

I look for more edible jewels, until I sense a presence other than my own. Someone shod in moccasins is following me. I hear these moccasins touch dirt, like animal paws. I realize they're too soft--sneaky-soft, they close in on me. I walk faster, my back soldierly straight, but somehow vulnerable, like a scraped cut.

When I walk faster, so do these paws and the taste I detected turns into the mold rocks harvest. This moldy taste grows stronger, pastier, mixes in with the scent of my growing fear. This feral fear snaps in the air about my face, like static electricity, or the shimmery place in a flame-tip.

These woods I wander with wanton abandon shift when I perceive how this threat scouts me in my Scout uniform. Twigs, small as matches, *snap*, until I stop, stock-still, pivot to see who's following me on sneaky-soft paws.

An unmanly man stands several squeamish inches apart from me. Is he a boy-man, trying on how to be an unmanly man made dark? Why would he sneak up on me, Little Bits?

I stand there in my Scout uniform, feel how thin I am, how easily my twig-bones would break. This man, tall as a priest, lords over me. His beard stubble is bristly, hoary, as his bee-bee eyes, like Mom's, tighten.

"How old are you?" he demands in Father's businessman voice.

"Ten," I reply, "ten going on eleven."

"Take off your clothes," he groans in a groan sounding too familiar to me.

"No," I snap in a scrappy voice, "I won't."

"Take off your clothes," he demands again. It's then I see his giant slingshot, big as a black mechanical insect. It's loaded with a motherlode of a stone. Its tension fires in my synapses.

My synapses fire as I realize this man is Goliath and I'm David, only this Goliath possesses the sling shot I sorely need. I make my voice storm the woods. "I'm David," I pronounce. My fury unfurls frost fire up my spine, "You, Goliath, aren't allowed to hurt me." I storm again, "You aren't allowed to hurt me," just as I had at Father in my Playhouse not that long ago.

Goliath snorts, "Little bitch."

"Am not," I snort back as this bitch of a David turns, flees. The motherlode stone whizzes by my hip, followed by another, another, as I rip through brambles that tear my Scout uniform until my badge sash is bloody, especially my scribe badge with its feathery pen. I run between trees older than I'll ever be, through corridors of sticky webs whose threads plaster my hair and eyelashes. My Goliath has not harmed me.

Unharmed, I run home and as I run, I'm no longer David, but Little Bits. As such, I tear into the house, right through the kitchen where Mom's eating a chocolate sundae. I hear her cards slap down on the table in an endless game of Solitaire. On the radio, Paul Harvey says, "Good day." Ripping past her, I go up into her bedroom, straight across the royal red carpeting and into the closet where Mom undresses each night, her torso turning like a twisted, bitter root. In that closet, I stand, shivering, grow nocturnal, let bats whistle their deadly joy through my ears.

Eventually, I go to Mother, tell her what happened.

"Who was he?" she demands while a vein throbs on her right temple. Her blood starts to have a trickle-down effect in me.

"I don't know," I reply.

She drags me into the car, guns it, backfires, then drives fiendishly fast over to the woods. She yanks me along as we scour them.

"Where is he?" she yells, as furiously as had I at my Goliath.

"Where the hell is he?" Her rage mixes in that flame-tip of order and turbulence.

"I don't know," I say, "I just don't know."

We look everywhere, but Goliath is gone. We drive home. Mommy's cursing under her breath. Is she cursing me, or that unmanly man? It has to be me because if that man's nowhere to be seen, he never existed.

I *do* exist, willingly or not. When we get home, I'm sent to my room. I obey, sit there, far too alone for too long a time. Mother busies herself by smacking houseflies with the rolled-up newspaper she uses to frighten our pets into submission. *Thwack, thwack,* goes that rolled-up newspaper. It thuds like her once thundering, blundering blows.

Thwack. I hide in my closet, like one of our frightened pets. For decades, I'll wander that house, calling to those animals in hiding, hoping they'll come out, but the alphabet of loss mixes up the letters until it is my son's name I hear, a son I'll come to bear in glory, yes, it's Ryan's name I hear, like a prayer that comes from the grave.

XII.
LITTLE BITS BURIES A TIME CAPSULE

One Sunday after Mass, Dad takes us on a family drive. We climb into his cigar box brown sedan, half the size of a small house. We climb in, like boat people ready to ferry over the prairies that've been scalped from our landscape. Where we might go is a question that bobs above our heads, like empty word balloons.

Dad starts up the driveway, leaving behind our wine-dark, split-level house. We leave behind Mom's clutch of cranky marigolds and dandelions whose fluff matches the chapel veil still bobby-pinned to my short, brown hair. We leave behind a plum tree whose shed blossoms have long since fallen, shed blossoms that no one can rake up.

"Dad," I say, "we need to stop. Fred is following us." I'm watching my little dog chase the car from the rear window where I'm kneeling on the vinyl seat.

Dad draws in his humid breath. The world halts. Fred keeps running after the car.

He's skirting the rear wheels. "Dad, stop!" I yell, but he doesn't even reach for the brake. I hear a loud crunch, like an acorn with an ocean inside it. Then, only then, does my father stop.

I lunge out of the car. Fred's head is crushed, like that acorn, but the ocean inside it is a sea of blood. My little dog is dead. Danny, Marie and Gene gawk at me through car windows gleaming with a gunmetal sheen. Mother doesn't even turn her head--it's topped by the thorny nest of her church hat. She simply pulls down its black, spidery veil.

I tear into the woods, my migrating woods where I, Little Bits, stand among stripling maples, shaking, like their stripling leaves. Here, there are no catkin fairies dingle-dangling on the twigs, or slinky sea-green inch worms. There's just me, shaking like the maple leaves because Dad has run over my little dog.

I remain here, shaking, among trees, thin as whippets. I remain here until I start to calm down. As I calm down, I walk deeper into the woods. I walk into its homemade brewery of sweetness, its scent of molasses-soaked hay. I walk, leaving a wake of sorrow behind me for my dog, who'll never be mentioned again. As I leave my sorrow behind, I walk out of my girlhood. I walk out of my girlhood into my ever-inflating angelness. This angel-ness is my trueness, akin to the true lines of a house, especially of one by the sea.

In the woods, my wake of sorrow turns into succor. I pause, cup my hands to drink in my succor. I begin to feel that nothing can harm me, not the dark stilts of trees, nor the caterpillar dung scattered like an elite ellipses, or the black crows flying like shadow puppets in the canopy. I understand that my Goliath is gone and therein rest, templed by own pervasive quiet, its steep deepness, while noting how I'm that smudge of iridescence gleaming in a tree snail, or the patent leather spots on ladybugs. I bend over, ask, *red dew, red dew, who's hardened you?*

Perfect in my trueness, I curtsy before licorice wounds incised in trees, write on peels of birch bark, kiss the churlish pinecones until they're tipsy, then listen to the ocean inside acorns. I can't help but love how my sorrow turns everything into succor and how thoroughly that succor nourishes me.

I keep walking out of my girlhood, until I get to the Sinnissippi Bandstand in the middle of the woods. Here I fashion, then bury a time capsule. I take a hollow piece of wood, stuff it with the mosses I enshrine tree stumps with, add in my mood ring and the magic beans I always keep in my pockets. I kneel, dig a hole with my bare hands. I put the time capsule into the hole, blanket it with my chapel veil, then sprinkle fairy dust all over it before covering it with soil soft as the chamois lining the pockets of my father's favorite cardigan, the one I always wear, even though he yells at me for doing so.

How else can I keep the Midwestern chill--a chill that's screeching cold in winter, one that even wells up from the groundswell in summer, from adhering to my twig-bones without wearing my father's favorite cardigan? I can't, so I steal it from his bureau, not caring when he yells at me.

In this cardigan I'll come to watch my father burning the leaves, year after year, the ones that fall from the stately oak outside my triptych bedroom windows. The leaves fall, like torn-up grocery bags, from that oak until Father burns them. As I listen to crickets, I see the orange flame, the smoke, the rake he leans on in twilight. The woods are awash with these crickets, each like a shiny bow for a doll's hair. They're awash with the music I'm meant to perform on earth, music silky as my cornsilk insides and the memory of spring grass. The weave this music casts upon me will remain in the opera of the dark life, in each happiness of every day.

Years after Dad's death, I remain in an opera, yet not of the dark life, while composing the drifty language shimmed between heart and mind, the entities within and without, knowing the dead send messages like this, through walls into soul. I long to catch each word, each pause-in-breath, like loose moths in lamplight. I live to call these words out in watermarked ribbons of language, then let the earth's response spool beneath my ribcage.

I do not call to my Father, nor do I whisper his name, like things said at Mass, things meant to not be remembered. Nor do I call to Mother. Rather, I let their dead souls remain in that wine-dark house, which like a seashell waked from Sea Point Beach, echoes the eerie abstractions of time. I see my old chenille bedspread, the fish in the tank whose flesh, if touched, would shower a thousand golden scales. There I also see my parents, twitching like marionettes hung in the background.

Once they had young faces and understood the wildness hearts cave under, the craft love manifests before it goes asunder. Who, then, choreographed the three of us, their lead which I refused to follow? What then, is sadder? Not to be sad is to deny the transgressions they levied against me, the downed leaves, the wakened bones in my own waking body. It is to deny the dreams sorting through myth and magic, the magic sorting through life and loneliness as I once did their possessions when newly dead.

As I rub my father's sweater, I can still smell him, burning the leaves, year after year. I smell the saffron flame, the curlicued smoke. I see the rake he leans on in twilight, the rake of his hands, the rake of his body, the scrape it made down my body, its scar, newly healed, like a cocoon from which a hundred thousand monarchs shall, do migrate.

XIII.
LITTLE BITS GETS A LIFE

I'm gawking at dozens of chick eggs in the incubator at The Museum of Science and Industry in Chicago. I stare at these eggs, like dozens of pool balls on white felt, knowing each one of them is generating new cells. I, too, am generating new cells, like scabs on boo-boos, scabs hard as the shells of these chick eggs. I wonder: do the eggs have tiny snow globes in them, Egyptian jewels, hand sewn lace? Are they filled with lemon chiffon, sealing wax, or a jawbreaker? Will the eggs arrange themselves in a mystic circle and does heaven hang upside-down in them?

I keep my fingertips pressed--edge-lit, red, nubile as salamanders--against the glass, longing to crawl inside that incubator, to be in the heaven hanging upside-down in the chick eggs. I hear the delicate drilling of tiny pickaxes working inside them. *Peck-peck, peck-peck.* A fault line appears, followed by another, then another. *Peck-peck.*

Soon, a shell, thin as doll china, shatters and a beak peeps out, like a miniature horn of cornucopia, followed by yellow fuzz, bristly as pipe cleaner. Other beaks peep out, more yellow fuzz, then here a foot, there a foot, everywhere a foot, foot. Chicks emerge, slick with birth grease--pathetic, scrawny things, just like me. The chicks tick with seed, are wet, downy sunflowers with tiny brown eyes. I, too, tick with seed, have dark, tiny eyes and downy hair. I deem this likeness to be good.

The incubator is a hothouse, yet not for flowers, but hothouse babies. I want to be a hothouse baby, grow strong in twelve different ways, not be the Little Bits I am, yet to be Little Bits is to know that human time isn't chick time, nor is chick time kangaroo time and kangaroo time isn't atomic time or ant time. All times happen simultaneously, they elide--turtle time, rock time, wind time, warp time.

If I were in chick time, I, too, would slip through a gooey membrane into a sweet translucence. I, too, would pass through that translucence, only to *peck-peck* at layers of my own shell, as though it were full of love's vast sea.

And if I were full of love's vast sea--*I am!*--that means I can't be emptied. It means I can hear high tide with its voluminous bass bravado, as well as the crinkly silks of low tide stirring pebbles, like tiny stone eggs. I, too, can peel off layers of my shell, as if stripping away the crunchy veils, cellophanes and elusive, yet musical slips of my existence. I peel and peel until all I hold is a slippery fetal orb, a wet eye. I press this wet eye to my forehead until my seeing becomes vast, oracular.

This vast seeing starts to happen as Mom jerks me away from the glass. The rest of the family is with her. We all exit down the museum's stone steps, as my oracular seeing imbibes autumn, stolid lampposts, cold, steely rain. My seeing perceives that this cold rain makes sad puddles. Within them, heaven hangs upside-down. My seeing sees the elegant hem that dresses love's vast sea, the one which labors to build us with the same beauty, one bound by the failings of flesh, which abide, abide, until swiftly doth come our demise.

This seeing is voracious, yet airy as the autumnal grace that flows in errant avenues with breathy ease as we steel ourselves for another freezing, barren Midwestern winter. My seeing *cut, cuts* like Father's jack knife once did into my shoulder blades. When it *cuts* it becomes wounded seeing. Because I'm not in kangaroo time or atomic time, my wounded seeing sees how wounded everything is--from the black, galactic potholes, to the pock marks in air and Father's cold hands, the color of damaged mulberries.

As we walk toward the car, I feel like one created for this seeing, for my furiously beautiful visions, which makes cherries ache from the inside-out. Why else did Mom, over breakfast, shove the newspaper across the table to where I was eating my cinnamon toast, only to rap her index finger pointedly on a photo of a child fed only newspaper, teaspoons of water? Was she warning me? Was she insisting that I count my blessings? Would this starving child have to keep growing new cells, like scabs on boo-boos, scabs hard as the shells on chick eggs, just like me?

We kids now pile into the brown sedan, half the size of a small house, for the drive back to Rockford. Mother hands out milk cartons from the front seat. Dad drives while I suck on the milk through a straw bent, like a pipe cleaner, only to see myself on the carton, there in the picture of the missing child plastered on its back. This girl's eyes have sunk into their sockets. She has a faraway look, as though no longer in any kind of imaginable time, human or otherwise. She just looks lost in the cold, lonesome prairies of unclaimed outer space. How can I not float with her, a tiny astronaut untethered from the Mother ship? Or have I, Little Bits, always floated with her in those cold acres of space?

As I suck on my milk like the missing person I am, we drive by miles and miles of frozen, lonesome prairie. Most of this prairie's been tilled into farm land where the corn stubble looks as rough as Dad's beard stubble. I turn over the story he's just told us about another missing person, my great grandfather, Charlie, who walked out on my great grandmother, Lizzie, in turn-of-the-century New York. He also walked out on three young children.

I imagine a tenement walk-up on a sooty evening, the black, ominous lanterns not yet lit. Maybe the walk-up's on the third floor, diapers strung out the bathroom window like dingy prayer flags. There are three rooms and my great grandfather holds onto a glass doorknob as he steps through the heavy, mahogany door. He's stepping out to get the paper or cigarettes. He's stepping out to get a life because that's what we Kirschners do. We yell, "Why don't you get a life?" when angry, as though it were possible to be alive and not have one. *Get a life*. Charlie did just that.

When my great grandpa, Charlie, went to get a life, he left behind an iron bed covered by bald grey blankets, a bureau with a yellowed lace doily, one old bottle of perfume emptied of its burnished oil. He left behind a low sofa shoved beneath large, ghostly windows, two small children on a cold, bare floor banging spoons on dented metal cups and my great grandmother, Lizzie, as she came out of the tiny bathroom after washing those dirty diaper prayer flags. Baby cocked on her hip, she wasn't yet thinking, *Where's Charlie?* Instead, she started to heat some water in a kettle to bathe that baby with, in the kitchen sink, while wondering how to make enough soup with a ham bone, two bug-eyed potatoes, a carrot thin as her wrists. An old tune arose in those destitute rooms, *Even my poor kettle is singing the blues for you.*

Although Lizzie may have found Charlie's disappearance mystifying, even disorienting, there would be nothing to do about it other than to get by, so her children could. What did she do--sew for a little money? Iron? Wasn't the phrase, *how to feed?* the grind in her mind and not, *where's Charlie?* Gone is gone. People vanish and I never did learn what became of my namesake, or her children, except for my paternal grandfather, Caspar.

Caspar was husband to Grandma, Edwina, mother of three: my father, Uncle Ed, Aunt Anne. Driving, Dad says, "Your grandfather was a piano tuner before the Great Depression," and I picture his long, spooky piano tuner fingers, boney as hand rakes. "We lived in Flushing and were poor as church mice," Dad goes on, his voice nearly lilting. "When the Depression hit, no one could afford to tune their pianos, so Grandpa refereed boxing matches." Dad straightens up, as though sitting tall in the saddle as he adds, "He coached the Golden Gloves."

While my brothers and sister let out low whistles to show how impressed they are, I see Caspar in ring after smoky ring, under a sickly bare lightbulb, separating fuming boxers, snorting like bulls, or doing the countdown while shooting out those spooky piano tuner fingers--*down for one, two, three, you're out.* Did he snort and fume, like a bull, at his own children? Did he darkly father my own dark father?

Dad continues, "After the boxing matches, I fetched your grandpa nickel pails of beer, even though I was just a boy."

I figure Dad fetched many nickel pails of beer for my grandpa, hauling them up how many rickety steps to the small hovel they barely got by in. I hear the beer slosh, like slop for pigs, and Dad sucking down his portion of that bubbly broth. Did those empty pails give them all a pot to piss in? Did Caspar use them as spittoons?

"That's it," Dad says, and we all know this means *end of story.* How and when Caspar died is and will remain a mystery to not just me, but all us kids, as Dad and Mom are want to define mystery as that which isn't to be talked about. *At all.* This is why I'll never know if violence was levied upon them as children which they, in turn, levied upon me.

Dad's family story, of course, doesn't end with the mysterious demise of my grandfather, even though he died before I was born. There's one more piece. We're back in the Great Depression and my grandparents are very poor. They were poor before the Depression, so the poverty is abject.

"Guess what?" I say to Ryan as we lolly-gag in kayaks on Spruce Creek. The leaves on nearby trees look like green wax, the sky, caloric with light.

"What Mom?" he says lazily. Ryan's legs are too long for the kayak, so he appears to be squished into Mother Hubbard's shoe.

"Did I ever tell you what became of my great grandpa, Charlie, after he disappeared on Lizzie?"

"No," he says, while studying the dimples in the water.

"Well, no one heard a thing about him until he died. Guess where he kicked over?"

"Where Mom?" Ryan looks like he's gone fishing even though he hasn't.

"The Waldorf Astoria. He'd been living there for years."

Ryan lifts one eyebrow. It's the color of the sunfish he may have gone fishing for.

"And?"

"Turns out he was a famous bookie in New York City. He was known as 'Racehorse Charlie'."

The other eyebrow goes up. "Really?"

"Yep. Racehorse Charlie left a heap of money to my grandpa, Caspar. The will was contested by the doorman at the Waldorf. The doorman lost."

Ryan smiles. Anything remotely shady interests him and no one's about to deny that Racehorse Charlie isn't shady, so I add, "I bet you didn't know there's a famous bookie in the family tree."

"Nope," he says, positively beaming now.

We keep paddling as I tell him how Caspar took that money and bought a new car. In the Depression. *With cash.* I tell him how Caspar also used that money to send my father, then Uncle Ed, to college, the first ever in my family.

"Dad was at Lehigh not long after Herbert was at Lafayette," I continue. Herbert was Ryan's paternal grandfather. Donald went to Lafayette, too, so that the fact my father was a Lehigh man and the Frost's were Lafayette men was a source of horror to them, as was my being poor as a church mouse. I never did tell them about the food stamps.

"Thank goodness," I add, "you chose not to go to Lafayette. Three generations of Frosts at that school would've been too much."

"Tell me about it," Ryan says, "and you know who was dead set on my going."

"I know, I know," I answer, but my thoughts are starting to drift. So are the kayaks. As we glide down Spruce Creek, I elide back in time to school nights in Rockford. I'm back in the car, that cigar box brown sedan, with Dad. He's driving to the office. Most nights, he goes back to the office and if I'm a good girl, I get to go with him to do my homework.

We're crossing the Rock River, fat and swollen as a snake who's just swallowed a mouse, big as a gopher. There's a bike path along that river. It's the one Mother and I walk on with the Walkie-Talkies, donned in our sneakers with the fluorescent orange shoe strings. I like walking with Mom and the Walkie-Talkies as much as I like going back to the office with Dad. Both make me feel grownup. Briefly, I get to be someone other than Little Bits. I get to get a life.

Father's office is in a modern building. When we enter the lobby, he points to a painting that looks like a red bull's-eye. "Now, Little Bits, there's a piece of abstract art for you," he says with the assurance of the collector he isn't. Somehow the sad clown painting, which now hangs in the family room, doesn't strike me as a collector's item, but then I may not be one either.

A lucky rabbit's foot, maybe, but not a collector's item because somewhere, in the cold storage drawer of the memories I don't yet remember, Dad said, "You're my lucky rabbit's foot," while creeping on me. He petted and petted until I was nearly petted to death.

Lucky rabbit's foot or not, I follow Dad as he leads me over to the library where I'm allowed to look at Time-Life Books once I finish my homework. While I scrawl out my numbers, a huge furnace *whirs*, groans, almost tenderly. From time to time, I look up to see Dad, as he works with red pencil, soft as crayon, in the columns of an industrial ledger. He works his red pencil in the columns of the ledger, groans, almost tenderly--*wet dreams, wet savior.*

The furnace stops whirring. A single teardrop wrenches itself from the water cooler's glass skull--*wet dreams, wet savior.* I close my book. It's time to go home.

Back at home, I climb into bed, cold as an altar slab. I dread bed. I dread it because of the nightmares. Snared by them, over and over, I'm closeted in my bedroom which is, by extension, my world. Sleety, buzzing and cold, this world mimics the silence which steels over our freezing, barren Midwestern winters.

In perennial darkness, I stare out my triptych of windows at leaves the color of torn-up grocery bags. They tatter the frostbitten ground beneath the old stately oak, scuttle in wind-gusts like ghost crabs. I long to hang jack-o-lanterns on branches handcuffed by icy bracelets, but gawk, instead, at flatness--annihilating, billboard flatness while winds screech down the prowling landscape.

This prowling is inescapable, the winds go after it, like a predator. While it prowls, I lay billboard-stiff on my bed, shuttle into nightmares. I dream about Queen Elizabeth, dead for five hundred years, fear my eye-hollows, like hers, are caves devoid of moonmilk. Our bodies are pieces of petrified wood. As I lay under my thin, chenille bedspread, I'm the tip of an iceberg, or a paralytic, unable to lift a finger, twitch a toe.

I'm wide-awake in my paralytic state. The room rocks, a crazy crypt. It rocks back and forth, up, then down, becomes a seasick ship where I can't launch a mutiny. My body fluids slosh as the room rocks, slowly then faster--it changes speeds, lickety-split, pitches high, then low, low, way below sea level where primitive bottom fish scrub me with shelf-fungi scales, pinking-sheered fins.

The room not only rocks, it changes sizes. One minute it's a skyscraper, the next, a matchbox from Father's matchbox collection, then it's a big, old barn, or a baby's tight, white casket. I, too, change sizes, am stretched out into a stretcher that stretchers into years before being squashed in a vise. The room smells of snuff peppered by snow whose tiny flakes are blue, antique toys.

This is my room, and by extension, my world. Purple poodles with bouffant hairdos powder their noses before purple mirrors on the wallpaper, then turn into rabid dogs barking like hellhounds. While they bark like hellhounds, my paralytic state begins to subside. I get up to escape my room, my rocking, ever-changing sizes room, creep across the hallway, only to ball up at the foot of Mother and Father's door, like an icy bug in a wintering-over web. This is my world and by extension, my life.

It's my life until I, Little Bits, in little over a decade, decide to get a life. I get a life by packing up everything I own into a sedan, brown as a cigar box, to move to the very seacoast where, decades later, I'll return to get a life once more. I'll return by packing up everything I own in another car, half the size of a small house, to live in my Sea Cabin. I get a life alright, but not being a famous bookie, but by remaining that shadier thing, a poet who writes books.

Ryan gently starts to rock my kayak, "Mo-m," he says, "where are you? You've got that faraway look in your eyes."

I straighten up, "Here," I reply, "right here. And you know why?"

"Why?" he asks.

"Because heaven's here, nine times out of ten."

Ryan says, "I remember when you used to say, *fall down ten times, get up eleven.*" I know he's referring to the seizure years, when I did fall down not just ten, but hundreds of times, only to get back up hundreds of more times.

"Knowing how to fall may be an art form," I reply, "but this is much better."

He smiles, "I think I get it. It's like heaven's here in this dimple of water. Kind of hanging upside-down, but here."

"Absolutely," I reply, "it's even hanging in your eyes."

Ryan dips his paddle in the water, as if anointing it. "Okay, let's go home now to work on our book lists. I'm worried I won't I get to read them all before I die."

I resist telling him not to worry because he's only twenty by saying, "Honey, some people have bucket lists, we have book lists."

I then anoint my paddle in the water, let the heaven that's here slide under me, over and through me until I start to grow new cells, to incubate them in the hothouse of my body because that's what bodies do, as we're all built with the same beauty in mind, a beauty bound by the failings of flesh, abiding, abiding until swiftly doth come our demise.

XIV.
LITTLE BITS' PERFECT SUICIDE DIVE

I climb up the cold steel ladder that leads to the high dive. It's summer in Rockford and I'm at the J.C.C.'s outdoor pool. I climb all the way up the ladder, then out onto the diving board. From here, I see the aqua pool below, swimmers bobbing like eggs. I see the patch of woods, its tuft of green fur, that separates the pool from our house. I expect my troll dolls to march out of the woods's wooly tuft, troll dolls I dress in cavemen clothes sewn from emerald mosses.

I note earth from a high point of view, then walk to the end of the high dive to prepare for my suicide dive, which isn't a belly flop, nor a can opener or cannonball. Anybody can do those feats, but I'm going to execute the perfect suicide dive. Turning my back to the swimmers below, I measure out the three steps I need to make a proper approach. I pivot, make that approach, each step a bit faster than the last. My arms come up over my head to gain momentum, so I can spring off the board and achieve the height necessary to perform my suicide dive.

After springing off the high dive, I'm airborne, suspended in time and space, but what am I diving into? Water cool as a cube? An inviolable maw?

Suspended, I arch back in a reverse swan dive toward the board I've leapt from. Back arched, my toes are pointed, my arms stretched into a taut capital "T," which stands for *trouble,* yet form matters, trouble or not. I'll be judged by the perfection of my form while suspended in time and space.

As I hurl backward toward the board in my reverse swan dive, my body is goose-pimply. The edge of the diving board whizzes by my face. This is what makes it a suicide dive. As my tight body streaks toward the water below, I'm flying, fast. I'm splendidly spilling, splendidly alive as I streak toward the water below with my taut belly facing the wide, blue sky.

For a moment, brief as grace, I'm spilling, splendidly alive, streaking in my goose-pimply body. I'm also a fluid mass of flesh fluidly falling in my suicide dive. I'm a fluid mass falling in my suicide dive as I slip into the water, like Cinderella's foot into its glass slipper.

Only my slipper isn't glass, it's water cool as a cube. My slipping into this watery slipper without a splash is proof that I've perfectly executed my dive. Now the water churns, makes great muscular clouds. Chlorine stings, like jelly fish, while I'm propelled, an underwater waterfall, to the bottom of the eleven foot deep end with far too much speed and velocity. As I'm propelled to the bottom of the eleven foot deep end, I knife through these muscular clouds.

Arms stretched, I hear the water tear seams while the churning becomes a cerulean underworld. The bottom of this underworld is rapidly approaching, hard as a cement bunker. When I hit this bunker, will I detonate, like a fleshy bullet producing mushroom clouds of blood? Or am I a sleek nuclear sub whose *boom* will rocket other swimmers out of the pool? Will this subatomic heat hard-boil us all, like a clutch of chick eggs?

My hands touch down first, to slow the velocity, then my feet follow until I squat, a primitive goddess, only to push off that bunker without detonating. How can this be? How could I have not *boomed* at the bottom of this cerulean world? I don't know. I just push off that bottom with great force. When I push off, my swimsuit straps snap.

When my straps snap, I'm naked from the waist up. I'm running out of breath in my underwater waterfall--my lungs burn and I kick my flipper feet, hard, to get to the water's surface. My lungs burn as I kick my feet hard to get, half-naked, to the water's surface, which is magnified by light, lip-lidded and metallic. When I explode through this lip-lidded light, I break through its iron petals, am a muscle of infinite reception.

Applause explodes as I break through the surface to see that my flipper feet have fused into a tail. It's speckled with glittery scales.

"I'm a mermaid," I yell, "I'm not Little Bits, but a mermaid!"

I spy Mom. She's bug-eyed with horror.

"Mermaid," I yell, "a real live mermaid," while bounding out of the pool so all my scales can glitter in the metallic light.

Mom's bug-eyed horror makes me stupidly happy, even as she runs into the pool area to throw a wet towel over me, but before she can throw that wet towel over me, I glance at the judges scores: *ten, ten, ten.*

XV.
GRANDMA IN THE OLD FOLKS HOME

"Why does Grandma have to go into the Old Folks Home?" I ask. "Can't she just live with us, down in the den? That's her high bed, after all."

Mom and Dad roll their eyes. "She's old," they reply in unison, then clink the ice in their cocktail glasses.

"But," I start, "Grandma could do the ironing and mending. Besides, she and I make wicked-good manna pancakes."

Dad pulls down the rim of his golf hat. "How'd you do on the back nine, Ad?" This is a serious, nearly religious question, one that excludes me and Grandma.

"Should have used an iron on ten, lost a ball in the woods on thirteen, but was par for seventeen and eighteen," she answers, her face wreathed in cigarette smoke.

Father whistles through his teeth, then pulls on his own cigarette. Smoke scuds across the ceiling of the screened-in porch. "Don't want to talk about my game," he says in a low voice.

"Then don't," says Mother. Both of them look like clay figures dipped in oil paint.

"I blew the paper account today," he adds in an even lower voice while he toys with his pant zipper, like the silver tongue of a snake.

"You what?" she yells while snatching at her hair as if it's filled with static electricity.

"The paper account," Dad murmurs in a voice that's the lowest of lowly.

Boom, I hear, *boom, boom,* early fireworks fill the sky--*blue roar, red applause*--as Mom blasts Dad. I slip away.

I feel sad, but Grandma is put in the Old Folks Home anyway. Saddened, I go visit her everyday after school. Her room's like the inside of a tissue box, smells of mashed apples. Tissue-thin walls seem to absorb Grandma's tears, tears pulled from her eyes, just to leap with a thousand others.

I kiss her, cross over to the bureau. There, I lift out one of her hand-embroidered hankies, moisten it with rosewater, dab her forehead and cheeks to rid her of the mashed apples smell.

"Grandma," I intone, "it's me, your Guardian Angel."

Grandma tries to smile, but it lacks her insider radiance. I take out sheets of Japanese paper to record letters for her. The paper is thin, translucent, as is her lilac-tinted skin.

"How about Aunt Rita?" I suggest, "why don't we write her? You've always said Aunt Rita has a hotline to heaven. Maybe she'll offer a Novena for you."

Grandma folds one hand over the other, like tea napkins. Her sapphire eyes are pale, mute as sail cloth.

"Grandma," I repeat, "it's me, your Guardian Angel," but her lilac face only grows thinner than the translucent Japanese paper I'm poised to write on.

"Grandma," I plead, "you must remember your Guardian Angel." Her eyes gloss over. Wherever she is, it's unfathomable.

I persist, "Don't you remember the 1963 World's Fair where we walked everywhere, arm-in-arm, like two old sweethearts? We stood in the Wall of People and I got to shake hands with Carby Carburetor. He looked like the Tin Man and you took a picture of us with the Brownie camera, remember?"

Grandma doesn't, so I drop to my knees, place my head in her lap, the lap of my beloved, where it turns in leaden glory. I stay there a long time, in supplication.

When I get up, she slowly gestures to her coin purse, indicating I should take a quarter, as is our custom, for an ice cream cone. How can I when her own sweetness is being licked away until only the coarse salt in her bones remains. Coarse salt, bones, milk dust.

XVI.
ELIZABETH IN TORNADO COUNTRY

Older now, I become an Elizabeth, am no longer Little Bits. I play the piano while singing to Mother in late afternoon, in the rusting light, when the world slows down long enough to stop turning its Catherine wheel. I play a saraband all hot and bothered. The green leaves on trees hang so heavily, they sweat amber droplets. Ebony birds click their beaks as I stroke the ivories of the old black upright, a piano my piano-tuner grandfather might have tuned with his long, boney fingers, hard as hand rakes, the man who darkly fathered my own dark father.

Mom sinks deeply into the gold couch, sponged by my indigo notes as they seep into her bluesy pores. Behind her, my aquarium bubbles quietly. In it, the milky bodies of angel fish move, like the fast parts of stories, toward sudden, swift conclusions. Trailed by a rosary of feces, they drop capacious, torn veils.

I drop my own veil, its caul, while my decadent music moves like a nude descending the stairs. This nude descends, fluid as rain, pale as ale. In the rusting light of late afternoon, that nude descends, slow as luxury, almost a figment--my mother?--from another era. She descends while sifting sunlight threshes between her thighs. This figment pauses to imbibe my sultry notes, like a draught distilled from ginger and lemons. All around her, time weaves its spun gold until it's lengthened, sequestered by the cloistered hour.

The cloistered hour, impregnated by each of my hot, bothered notes, sequesters my mother and me, deeply, in the chamois afternoon. Sequestered in chamois afternoon, we sink like floaters until we are underwater in a private, voluminous library known only to us. I turn pages of sheet music--she turns pages of dreams, blank as flashcards. I sing to the silence walled within her sleep. I sing because music can't be caged, yet her body is a cage she's floated into, in the watery depths that holds us in our own private library.

Can my music bolt the cage my mother's floated into? I want her to remain in that cage, but she's an underwater waterfall, propelled by a violent velocity--no one can collect her, as she's more elusive than my music, which can't be caged. No one, not I, or the small god of her understanding will be able to bolt her cage, she who's bound to the physics of descent. I'm the one who's slipping from her, from her treacherous hold, from the deathly allure of her watery cage. I'm the one who rockets my motion into shape as I surge upward. As I surge upward, I see glittery, golden notes float on the surface like gingko leaves.

Propelled by the beauty of my music's churning propulsions, I plunge through the surface to float, bedecked with gingko leaves, with golden notes. The beauty of my music's propulsions extract me from my mother, like an essential oil, be it bergamot or lemon verbena. A dawning seeps into each of my pores: *my mother descends because she is deemed to.*

If she's deemed to descend, then my music choreographs that descent. Not only does she descend, but she also plunges into sleep, did so long ago--had I yet been born? She will always sleep as that's what she's sentenced herself to. I choreograph that sentence with my music. I sing in the late afternoon, in the rusting light as ebony birds click their beaks until the world stops turning its Catherine wheel, its Elizabeth wheel.

I go to Mother, to the gold couch she's sunk in. She's a book from our voluminous library, one filled with Biblical wrath, a perpetual literature of loss. I sit down, pull her head into my lap--its fetal, bulging, a world I can't open. Who would? Still, I leaf through her hair, its once black curls. My bones drift into the scene of her.

Although she's asleep, she pulls on me, like her cigarette. She pulls on me until my own papery insides glow, yet I want to be let go from her with a sadness I keep secret, like my middle name. All on earth wears it: the Mary birds, the Mary night, the Mary Mother.

Because I can't be let go from Mom, I turn to my music in love's vast sea until there's the end of her. At the end of her is the end of my night color, the color of a period on a page. It's the end of my music, which will be extracted from me, like an essential oil, until I come to live by the music of the sea.

For now, I mire her in my music because it is the work of daughters to do so. It is the work of daughters to choreograph their mothers' descent. She pulls on me some more while I mire her and sing. I not only sing to her mire in the rusting light of late afternoons, I also sing with Jack Sparks for Sister Grace.

In Chorus, Jack and I can't help but sing for Sister Grace. She's the magnetic force toward which every note is pulled, the way a tear is pulled from the eye, just to leap with a thousand others. There are others in Chorus, but they're lost in a blathering sea of sound in which only Jack and I are beacons. Our clarion voices swing like eye beams.

We sing in an underground classroom, cold as an elevator shaft, with ceiling tiles made out of cardboard, each square, a conquered country. The high school itself is a small city where the cold whooshes down its streets until our lips purple and chilblains grip our bones.

Nothing sparkles in our school except for the eyes of Sister Grace. These sparkles, minute as steely mica, are indestructible. From her, Jack Sparks and I learn the tonal range of angels about to fall into grace. When they do, we simply pitch our clarion voices higher, brighter. At first, Sister Grace teaches us the notes, then the notes on the page, after which she takes away the page, makes us sing right out into the air. We learn that our voices dwell beneath our breastbones, are wishing wells of breath which, when released, tingle our tonsils.

We sing for hours, our voices crisp as eidelweiss--we climb mountains with our voices, endure the loneliness of long distance runners. While we sing, anything's possible--stars pivot in our bodies and we script the air with fleur de lis.

Still, when Sister Grace snatches the last note out of the air and signals for us to stop, heavy machinery rolls in. This machinery has no girl or boy parts, no solos, altos nor tenors, or blonde sopranos.

Rather, it rolls over us with its rusting tonnage, flattens us into a billboard flatness that matches our landscape.

Sister Grace tours Jack and I around the state to sing to people ruined beyond belief, meek people whose meek eyes are squirrel-like and untrusting. These people, these sad mammals, gather in Grange Halls and VFW clubs to listen to the two of us pitch our voices, higher, brighter, until we hit an octave above heaven. Our mangy audience sits in metal folding chairs with their squat necks and backs molded into humps by hard labor in factories whose smoke hags our Midwestern skies. These forbidding souls fester in silence, like germs chomping themselves into pieces while we sing about a poor, wayfaring stranger, a motherless child. This is my youth, Jack's too, and by extension, our world, we who wield a willful need for dominance over the poor, the hideously broken, the God-fearing people God forgets about.

After these recitals in the rehearsal halls of the nearly dead, Sister Grace drives down blameless, nameless roads--we hover above them in her vehicle of transport so we won't be grimed by the sullied waste beneath us--oily feathers of crows, dark, dumbheaded nuts, seed keys blistering like ulcers.

On one such trip through a town that begs to be forgotten, just as I've forgotten everything, the winds come up with a strange, delectable desire that longs to run rampant. It turns the tender undersides of leaves into a rush of Pentecostal tongues. The sky seeps into green, yet not the green of emeralds, but one that's sickly, livid, somehow hooded. Sister Grace recognizes that sky. Jack and I recognize that sky--it grows gruesomely still, a stillness warped by danger. Moments later, a tornado touches down, like the tail of a giant black hornet. We fall to our knees on a sewer lid praying for mercy, mercy.

Mercy does not come as mercy is want to do--green, so much green, like bile, and the howl of that giant hornet blinds our senses as it yanks out roots, rips off roofs, blasts glass. Under that howl, a screaming occurs, frightful, panicked. This screaming is a Greek chorus of Medusa voices--it bolts into us, jolting us out of prayer and into the tornado's mania. We start to run--hard, fast, furiously--we're outrunning the tornado, its jumpy, indiscriminate, jigsaw path. We, too, are screaming in Medusa voices, join that Greek chorus, manic in our need to survive.

Then it halts. The tornado, which corkscrewed through the town leveling barns, flipping cars, gobbling tumbleweed and dreams and flattening everything that stood in its riff-raff way, screeches into an octave, not above heaven, but above a scream, and quickly vanishes.

The deathly, phosphorescent green sky grows opalescent while silence spreads its mantle over a land dismantled by the pitfalls and willfulness of jumpy destruction. Trailers have been wrecked like sixteen wheelers, bicycles spin dizzy wheels in trees, stalks of straw have been riveted, like Sebastian's arrows, into ripped-off siding. The dominance of destruction has prevailed--it always does--glorious and horrific. I see that horror has a holy aura. This aura veils our eerie landscape while Sister Grace, Jack and I wander about, lost in the seven circles of hell.

"This is nothing," I declare before fences pinned down by telephone poles, "nothing at all. You haven't seen anything yet." I want to go on, but it's not yet in my power to describe Mother and Father's willful devastation of my inner landscape. In my power is forgetfulness, which I've crafted to perfection in the low country of my imagination.

People have died in this tornado, cattle, too, chickens, sheep, horses. Farms, businesses, will go under and a whole bunch of ratty souls, including mine. This is no surprise in Tornado Country where nature, not love, reigns supreme. Here we all live in a natural order which is mostly disorderly, all mouth, like a mite whose greedy bite let's us know we're still alive.

XVII. ELIZABETH SUFFERS FROM AMNESIA TIMES TWO

When Jack Sparks and I aren't singing for Sister Grace, we drive back roads, hot tarry roads sealed to the land like grief. We drive by lonesome prairie, tilled into cornfields, out to rock quarries where we shoot beer cans. Here, I love the pull on the rifle, its kick, the blasphemous noise of bullets pummeling into cans and sheer rock face. This kick nearly knocks me off my feet, but I hold on, much like Mother does in her sorry garden patch when popping off squirrels. When she pops off squirrels, they fly up like pinwheels. I yell at her to stop, but she's determined to pop off any squirrel who might try to steal a sorry carrot from her sorry garden patch.

Now my own bullets, as do Jack's, blast stone until bits fly, like granite chips showering down the shoulders of the beautiful all. I aim at sheer rock face more than flimsy beer cans--my bullet holes are an illiterate alphabet only I understand, a symphony of violence as percussive as the blows Mom once smote upon me.

These bullets--mine, Jack's--thunder into boulders which know how to grow more than I do and we all know that stones can't grow, nor can bullets think. Rather, they sink to kill and the kill is everything, even if it's impossible to kill stone. My desire is to reduce the world to bits, as Mom and Dad reduced the Little Bits I was into something less than an it.

While riddling that quarry with bullets, Jack Sparks and I toss down beer after beer, kicking our heads back with each hearty guzzle. My now gloriously long hair is tied up, like an unruly mare's tail. The moon rises--a white cliff that's more shore than airy scape. It foretells the presence of a Mother other than the Mary Mother. She whispers to me: *your unravelling has begun.* Although my unraveling has begun, I still long for my once violated flesh to be stitched with clouds and flowers, with allusions to a more poetic universe. Instead, these stitches fall from my long blue dress. In its pleats, the printed wings of birds, whimper.

Beyond Jack Sparks and I, the cornfields seem Siberian, irresolute, inconsolable. I understand this in each of my wayward bones, draw in this desolation, its vast, ruptured sadness. This landscape maps me, like blue scars that can't be eradicated.

One night, as the stars thicken in the Mary sky, Jack Sparks and I, beery and full of glee, give each other plummy kisses in the back seat of my car. I let Jack Sparks drive down hot, tarry back roads sealed to the land like grief. I belt out, "Oh you, beautiful boy, what a beautiful boy you are," then roar with a dumb belly laugh.

Because one of the headlights is out, I cry, "Pididdle," which means I get another plummy kiss. As Jack plants that kiss on my cheek, the car veers, skids off the road, plows into pasture, hits solid berm. My cowboy-booted foot goes through the floorboard. My head smashes into glass, webbing it with a witchery of shattered lines.

When I come round, I don't remember my name, nor who Jack is. My mind is filled with a black mist that mystifies me. Although switches try to flip, none do. Together, Jack and I stagger to a nearby farmhouse, its Wyeth-like, tumbledown barn, damaged, dilapidated, like me.

We duck into this barn. Scrawny chickens, more pimpled than feathered, with red pomegranate asses, scratch at musky seed while doleful cows broadly low. Sheep, with faces marked like pansies, lay like a bunch of pickup sticks, upon heaps of broken straw. We nestle near them, unequipped to hold anything except each other. My amnesia overtakes me. I descend into sleep as frightfully deep as Mother's.

I wake to scratchy light shimming through barn boards, my head pounding the way it must have when whacked with the bat, but I don't remember anything, not Mother or Father, not even Jack. He rouses, recites my name like a Kabbalist prayer, but it means nothing, is a mere oddity of sounds. Only the pounding continues to pound in me while I suffer from amnesia times two.

While I suffer from amnesia--who's Elizabeth, who's Little Bits?--we give quiet thanks to the animals who watched over us as we slept and walk out of the barn. We note how the tarry back road has been buckled by last winter's frost heaves and the orneriness of the surrounding fields, unabashed in their ordinariness. Stubbled grasses are hardened from the inside-out, not only like Dad's beard stubble, but he himself. We reach the bend where my car went off the road. It has vanished.

Young, stupid, we hitchhike back to town. We hitchhike with surly truck drivers, sheathed in jeans, whose greasy bellies hang over cinched leather belts which have big, skull-like brass buckles.

Some of my amnesia subsides. Jack looks like a small animal in hiding while I gamble with these sordid truck drivers by pressing my warm finger into their thighs, then hissing like a cat. Shadows grow in my bones. If my head weren't pounding, I'd sing about how love is nothing but rock, salt and nails, yes, rock, salt and nails.

When Jack's left off at his house, he's a mere boy whose back retreats like a small, parched sail. When I swing out of the last truck at the top of my own driveway, my cowboy boots touch down onto the pavement where my little dog, some years before, had been run over by Father.

I walk down the driveway, opaque with dawn, in my cowboy boots and long, blue dress, serene as a bride. I wish for tappers on my boot bottoms so my feet could be percussive instruments. As I near the house, I see that the kitchen light's on. Nearer still, Mother and Father appear like Gothic apparitions by the sink. They're wrenching their hands, like cold, glass knobs. My feet may not be percussive, but my parents' voices are. As soon as I enter the house, they hit me with hard, fast staccatos.

"Young lady, where have you been?" starts Dad.

"Why didn't you call?" goes Mom, followed by, "We were worried sick."

"Your car was found in a ditch," yells he.

"We thought you were dead," goes she, then in a frog chorus they yell, "how could you do this to us?"

"Sorry," I say, "I had an accident, had amnesia. What was I supposed to do?"

"What the hell were you doing out in the middle of nowhere at three o'clock in the morning?" goes the frog chorus.

"Shooting beer cans in a rock quarry," I fire back.

"Shooting what?"

"Beer cans."

"Why?"

"Because I could," I say flatly.

Silence descends, a nearly disastrous silence. In that violent space, glares flare. *Because I could,* echoes in my pounding head, the one that smacked the windshield, shattering it into a witchery of webs. *Because I could* is what allowed my mother and father to perpetuate their violence upon the Little Bits I once was. *Because I could* is Nature's Anthem, especially here in Tornado Country where the dominance of destruction reigns supreme--it's the excuse we depend on, anything else is an untruth. *Because I could* is why I slam the kitchen door behind me, then tear up the stairs, leaving my parents behind me, very much behind me.

XVIII.
GRANDMA MOVES OUT OF HUMAN TIME FOR GOOD

I'm nineteen when Grandma moves out of human time for good. I drive home from college with Burgess, the young man I'm then living with. It's winter. All the ermine snow mantling the world's body holds my crystalized moments with Grandma. I remember how her hands once guided mine while we knitted so I wouldn't drop a stitch. Now snow drops these stitches--each is a letter in an illiterate alphabet only we understood. The heavy sky is a tapestry unraveling the way I'm unraveling.

I remember her apartment where I slept with her in her high bed under the pewter-colored, button-puckered comforter. I remember listening to her Wurlitzer whine like an old saint in a junkyard while waltzing with her to Lawrence Welk. Then there were those mornings when we made manna pancakes in her celestial green kitchen. Flour-clouds dusted the Little Bits I was until I became white as a pantomime. There's her garden, big as a storybook, her columbine, Japanese windflowers, red, red roses. As Burgess and I drive not in, but through winter, I'm sleepwalking my way toward her, arms outstretched--*Grandma, Grandma.*

When we arrive home, I'm told that she died alone, on the cold slab of an ambulance bed. During her move out of human time, did the Mary birds, full of charity and moonlight, fly out of her womb? Did their songs careen above the whine of the ambulance's sirens as each note fell, like a bright, silvery coin? I long to plunge my arms into the high banquet of those coins, to ascend with the Mary birds, but descend, instead, into the basement where Grandma's paltry belongings are spread out willy-nilly on the ping-pong table. While my family is upon on them, I touch her grey wig, old piano shawl, which like a prayer flag has hung in every hovel and home I've come to live in.

During that raw, marled night, Burgess wants me. We're in Grandma's high bed down in the den. He smells feral. I turn into a nocturnal animal, curl into a ball. He climbs on top of me, a predator upon prey. It's his genius to be a predator. I weep in an animal heap. Dark shanks of my hair get caught in my mouth. I can't stop weeping.

I cry, *I need to be Grandma's Guardian Angel.*

Burgess replies, *Babe, you're no angel,* but I just keep gnawing the shanks of my hair while weeping.

In the morning, Burgess goes out, buys me red, red roses. I take them while telling him to leave, *for good.* After he leaves, *for good,* I fondle petals, am back in my dream of Grandma's roses, which have fallen, simple as a stitch. I long to climb inside her womb, the one the Mary birds have flown out of, climb in, sleep, dream of red, red roses.

At the wake, she looks diminutive in her tent dress, her face small as a medal. Her coffin is a big, white shoe which is permanently walking away from me. Or so I believe. I'm only nineteen, after all. Little do I know how her balsam-scented spirit will become the air I breathe, day in, day out. Little do I know how the miraculous will re-create her in me because the miraculous is more defiant and willful than destruction--it's even more defiant than me.

At the funeral, more than people gather--the saints from all ages come, as does every single guardian angel, fallen or otherwise. I stand on my toes up on a choral riser in the cathedral's organ rafter, sing Grandma's favorite song.

"O happy day," I sing. Each syllable warbles, "O happy day," I sing, my voice birding, "when Jesus washed, when Jesus washed my sins away."

My voice isn't only a birding one, it's an amber voice full of Tibetan bells, dragonflies, petulant tongues. It's a shimmering voice, heavy as molten gold, bright as emerald mosses, one that has heft. As I sing, my soul, along with Grandma's, flies right out of the church with a big *whoosh* sound. My voice then pitches itself an octave above heaven, the heaven she's winging her way into while all the Mary birds sing with me, "O happy day! O happy day!"

XIX.
WALKING THE MOM

Nearly a year after Grandma's move out of human time, I'm home for the holidays. I'm home, but my brothers and sister aren't, so it's just me, Mom and Dad.

One night, I'm standing at one of the blue double sinks in the bathroom washing my face with Noxema. It's late--Mother staggers into the doorway, drunk.

"Why won't you talk to me?" she asks.

"I'm getting ready for bed," I answer, still slathering Noxema on my face, thick as pancake makeup.

"You never talk to me," Mom says, voice rising.

"Mom," I say, white-faced as a clown, "you know I don't like to talk to you when you've been drinking."

"I'm like Hemingway," she retorts, "I'm only good after a few drinks."

"And Hemingway blew his brains out," I cry.

Mother looks dazed, meekly terrified, but she's drunk, ghastly. I want to plead with her to sober up, but I'm angry in my clown-face--frightfully angry, so I don't. I'm angry and freezing cold, as I stand there in my thin, flannel nightgown with the abominable snowmen on it, the one I've worn since I was eight and is up to my elbows and knees. I shiver, feel my body temperature go down. Maybe my body temperature will go down so far, I'll enter a state of torpor, like Father did, and the chickadees do when the cold is so severe it's a bleak rebuke.

I want to enter a state of torpor, like the chickadees do, because the cold is rebuking me. I'm so cold, I feel stern, unrelenting. My entire being, at this moment, is a bleak rebuke, not just to Mom, but the entire world.

"You're crap," Mom says. She slurs her words the way I will with Donald, decades later.

"What?" I ask, stunned, but somehow I remember the Noxema smeared on my angry clown-face. Does she have coulphobia?

"You're crap," she repeats. "What's happened to you? You used to be the all-American girl, had everything going for you, but now?"

"What?"

"I'll tell you what," she pauses, as if to build up some steam. "You say you want to be a poet, whatever the hell that means, you dress like crap and ever since you broke up with that nice Burgess, you date crappy men. Besides, your hair's a rat's nest," she says, as she crosses her arms over her chest, then staggers as if she's been punched.

"I hate you." I say, even though I don't mean it. What I want to say is that I don't hate her, but it's hard, painful, to watch her destroy herself, as she once tried to destroy me. I want to say that I want to love her and need her to stop destroying herself, but I'm only twenty and she, Mom, is drunk, ghastly. Because I'm only twenty, I need a mom, who's not drunk. I need a mom who's not this mom, who's breaking my heart in the heart of the heart of the country.

Maybe, if my heart's breaking in the heart of the country, it means I'm still an all-American girl, just one whose all-American heart is broken. If I'm still an all-American girl, maybe I'm not crap, even though I do want to be a poet, wear crappy clothes, date crappy men, leave my long hair in a rat's nest.

Instead of telling her I love her, I say, "I long to hear the chickadees sing, but it's too damn cold. Don't you want to hear the chickadees sing, too?"

Mom says, "You're crazy." It's not the first time she's told me I'm crazy, nor will it be the last. She'll tell me I'm crazy until I marry Donald, who'll say it for her, especially after she dies her ghastly death.

Mother turns to leave. I almost start to sound the chickadee call--*chick-a-dee-dee-dee.* I almost sound the chickadee call because I long to love if not Mom, then myself, as much as I love the chickadees, but I don't, at least not yet. Nor do I sound the chickadee call because, like them, I'm cold, have entered a state of torpor.

In my torpor, I finish washing my face, my fingers, numb as a drum. I hear Mom thump from wall-to-wall down the hall to her room, like a sack of potatoes. I follow her, go into my room.

"Night," I say, to Mom and Dad, as if we're the Waltons.

Already pickled in cold, formaldehyde sleep, they don't answer. In torpor, I'm flat on my back in bed with the covers pulled up to my chin. My childhood nightmare returns. The room starts to change sizes--it grows small as a hatbox, or an infant's coffin, then big as a hearse for that coffin. It rocks from side to side, like a huge ship, while the purple poodles, with bouffant hairdos, powder their noses before purple mirrors and bark like hellhounds. Will this ever stop? My shape-shifting room, its incessant rocking, the hellish barking?

I put my foot down on the floor, like a drunk with the spinnies. For a moment, it all stops and when it does, I curl up, imagine myself cupped in a seashell. Is that the symbol for creativity? I like this thought, keep it near me as I started to drift into chick-a-dee-dee-sleep.

* * *

On Christmas Eve, we go out to Giovanni's for dinner. It's packed, as Italian restaurants are popular in Rockford. Here, the gauche wallpaper is dusty rose with a black, felt-raised pattern. Christmas lights are intertwined everywhere--around the windows and through the bannister that separates the bar from the dining room. We're seated at a little table along this divider. The waitress comes for drinks. I order a Coke. Mom and Dad, extra dry martinis.

"Well, here we are," says Dad.

I'm fingering the placemat, which has scallops along the edge when he adds, "What'll it be?"

"A large pizza," I reply.

"I want mushrooms," says Mother.

"Ad, you know I can't eat them."

"Little Bits," she says, "what do you want?"

I'm too old to be called Little Bits. She knows I'm an Elizabeth, but I let it slide. "I don't care," I say, "whatever Dad's having."

"Fine. We'll do half and half," he says.

"It's hot in here," says Mom.

"I'm freezing," I return while zipping up my parka.

Mother looks at me. "I'm sorry if you think I'm wrong. I can't stand the damn blower."

She lights up a cigarette. Dad does, too.

"You still cutting back?" I ask.

"Six a day," he replies.

"When he doesn't cheat," Mother puts in.

I let this slide, too, decide to go to the bathroom. Starting when I was just Little Bits, I always spent elaborate amounts of time in restaurant bathrooms, so much so, it became a family joke. I was mystified by the lounges at Stengos, the country club, even The Pink Pony and about a year ago, I marched Mother into the Men's Room at the Avalanche because there was a line for the Ladies. We broke into hysterics--Mom had never seen a urinal before. It got worse when I demonstrated how young men liked to stand far away and shoot their piss in an arc across the room, in order to pee on the bee, but old men huddled close, as if in a confessional, to dribble it down the drain.

When we came out, red-faced, giggling, the men in the bar were clearly perturbed.

By the time I get back to the table, the pizza has arrived. Mom's still smoking and working on another martini. An incoherent discussion follows about how the pizza is bad--it's my fault, and Dad's--because we're ganging up on her. Amid protestations and arguments, Mother gets on her coat, is gone.

"Another victory for alcohol," I murmur. Father eats the pizza, dribbling the cheese into his mouth. His face is purple from high blood pressure. He looks like death warmed over.

"Dad," I say, "we have to go get her. It's Christmas Eve, for God's sake, and it's snowing hard." It's also extremely cold and we're at least two miles from home.

After about ten minutes of stalling, he gives in. We drive the normal way home, on the main roads. Snow sticks to the black top as if to a cast. We don't see Mother anywhere. I snuggle deep in my parka, like the cocoon for a lime-green luna moth. Longing to be the final and fifth instar of that luna moth, I remember how one, large as a dinner plate, once appeared on, then disappeared from my bedroom window.

This lime-green luna moth appeared, disappeared, like the swift, dressy creation she was. Swift, dressy, she had lengthy, tapering hind wings, as well as sunflower-gold eye spots meant to confuse predators. As I snuggle in the cocoon of my parka, I, too, long for lengthy, hind wings, sorely need gold eye spots to confuse my predators. I long to pupate, to eclose at dawn, be a brief poetic preamble, just like her. Why wouldn't I want to live as a soft, green flare for a mere seven days, then mate in order to become the mistress of the mineral dark? Why wouldn't I want to be in the Saturnidae family and not the Kirschner one? How could I have known, at twenty, that all things Kirschnerize me, or that my own Kirschnerian Kyrie would eclose at dawn? How could I have known that once I did eclose, I'd pump body fluids into my lordly wings in order to take flight?

Because it's not possible, simply not possible, I continue to pupate until we arrive home. We haven't found Mom. Father beelines it into the house, straight to the bar where the liquor bottles glint like glassy idols.

"Dad," I call after him, "we need to find Mom." When he ignores me, I stop pupating, head down to the Rock River to search for her.

When I get to the Rock River, the night is licorice-black with a flinty after-bite of anise. Snow incubates more snow until each flake of its veritable thousands feels like a talisman. I long to stuff my pockets with these talismans as though they, like love, wouldn't vanish upon touch, but I'm searching for a human shape, albeit a wretched one, Mom.

In this barrage of snow-mirage along the Rock River, I call for her--a golden, shadowy call that the wind gulps down. I call for her again, golden, shadowy, while padding the air with my hands, as if to strip-search it for the wretched human shape that is Mom.

I get desperate. The licorice-black night is getting blacker. The veritable thousands bits of snow are maxing into millions. Feverish with flinty cold, I cry out, "Mommy, where are you?"

Groping in the snow-mirage, I cry again, "Mommy, where are you?" Has she fallen into the river, the one she walks along with the Walky-Talkies, the one I, too, walk along with her and the Walky-Talkies? Is she wearing the official Walky-Talkie sneakers with the florescent-orange shoelaces that glow-in-the-dark?

All that's glowing in this mineral darkness are the maxed-out millions of snowflakes. These maxed-out snowflakes, are brilliant, precocious as the Little Bits I once was. They seem to burn as they fall, like white fire. I'm afraid that this brilliant snow, this white fire, will ignite Mother. Or will my own white fire ignite her?

It doesn't. I make her out, stumbling like an old bear in the blizzard-fire. She's blindly pawing the precocious bits of maxed-out snow, the way I'll remember how Dad pawed me, as though I were a trench full of the darkest honey.

When I get closer, I hear Mom screaming. "Demons are attacking me," she yells, "get the demons off of me."

I yell back, "there are no demons."

She screams more, "The demons are in my hair." She paws at them, blindly, screaming, "they have red-and-black reptilian wings, are attacking full throttle."

"There are no demons," I yell, "I'm coming to get you."

When I get to her, I shake her. I shake her hard: is Mom so drunk she thinks demons are attacking her? I don't know, can't, until long after her ghastly death, her demons come to get me.

I shake her so hard, she's dazed. Dazed, she shakes her head, like a boxer. Is she about to go down? Does she hear my grandfather's count? Mother doesn't go down. Instead, she leans against my thin body, dizzied by the years-long blizzard in her dazed head.

"Baby steps, Mom, just take baby steps," I whisper. When she does, I realize I'm walking the Mom, baby step by baby step, in a sad pas de deux. Yes, I'm walking the Mom through all the darkness, cold and snow, step by step, in a sad pas de deux. I'm walking her through the years-long blizzard in her head while walking through the years-long blizzard in my own dazed head. We're both walking with winter, but I don't know it yet. We'll walk with winter until, baby step by baby step, we walk all the way home.

* * *

Next morning, when I enter the kitchen, Mom's sitting on her stool at the breakfast bar. She's sitting on her stool like a pauper, puppet, or the King's fool and it's Father who's king of this tawdry kingdom. Mother's smoking and drinking coffee from a smiley face mug.

Because I know what happened last night is a blackout in her blacked-out brain, I say, "Hi Mom," lightly, as if it could shim her up, but she hunkers down in her shrunken monkey body and her black eyes grow blacker, like dark grottoes.

"Have some coffee," she says, while waving across that stand of liquor bottles glinting like idols.

"No thanks," I say, then go over to bestow a kiss, light as a butterfly's, upon her leathery cheek. She flinches, as if struck.

"Why did you do that?" she asks, in a mouse's voice as it slips in a hole.

"It's Christmas," I reply, "that's why. 'Tis the season of joy and love."

I go over to the black upright piano, the one I'd played while singing as Mom slept her knocked-out sleep. Mom's corresponding silence was her almost thanks, which leant me a bit of pity.

I touch the keys, sing, "Silent Night," like a ballad. I play it slow, bluesy. I hear Mom sigh. Perhaps I'm playing for the child she once was, the one I studied in the photograph albums her mother had made for her, a woman whose only belief was that we're the victims of victims, she who prayed for us victims on her glow-in-the-dark rosary.

In those pages, Mother was dressed in ribbons and bows and her dark, curly hair was in luxurious abundance, curls that I wanted to bunch in my hands. Even now, I long to hold that child in my arms, like a living dolly. How, when did that girl vanish into the hag Mom before me, the Mom I walked home, step by step, in cold and darkness? I know I can't rescue her, but how about me? Hasn't the small god of her understanding abandoned her? Has he abandoned me?

Father starts to commandeer the kitchen by cooking runny, scrambled eggs, limp bacon. His eyes are bloodshot as he stares at Mom while she eats a half of a banana, her standard breakfast.

My hands lift from the keys. I long to play musical spoons, or the telephone game, but what message would I broadcast? *Love me like there's no tomorrow? Love me before putting one foot in grave?*

"Time for presents," I announce, then go on, "it's Christmas and Christmas is for giving." I walk over to the artificial tree, note how its growth has been stunted, as has mine. The ornaments are hanging on faux branches, bobbing like shiny eggs. I touch them gingerly, declare, "Christmas must be magical," knowing there's no magic at the center of our bleak existences.

I sit, Indian-style, on the blue shag rug, the one Mother rakes to keep neat. She follows suit, opens her legs in a victory "V" and holds open a plastic trash bag, ready to field the wads of wrapping paper Dad'll punt her way.

"Mom," I say, "this is for you," as I hand her a package. She rips it open, stares at my gift, her eyes stunned with tears.

"How could you?" she asks as she holds up the sampler I made for Grandma as a child, the one I'd sadly taken off the ping pong where her few possessions had been spread after her death.

"Bless this House O Lord we Pray," Mom whispers, as she reads the stitched words aloud while tracing the neat purple x's that form each letter. "You shouldn't have," she goes on, "it's too precious for me."

I go to her, hug her like a tree, one whose root ball has been packed so tight, its growth, like mine and the faux tree's, is stunted. "Happy Christmas," I say. Her grotto eyes well up again.

I turn to Dad. "This is for you," I say as I toss him his gift. He quickly unwraps it. A smile warps his lean, inelegant face. "Electric socks," he says, just like the king he is of this tawdry kingdom. "Thank you."

"I know your feet are always cold. These should help," I explain.

"I like warm tootsies," he says as he hands me my gift.

I sigh, can't imagine what's inside. I open it carefully, trying not to tear the paper, which has abominable snowmen on it, just like my old nightgown. I let out a cry when I lift out my gift. It's Father's favorite cardigan sweater, the one with suede elbow patches, chamois-lined pockets, leather buttons.

"Dad," I say, "I can't believe you're giving this to me." Truth is, I can't. This is the sweater I'd stolen from his bureau, for years, to wear around the house to keep the cold at bay, the one he scolded me for taking, insisting I stay out of his stuff. I stole it anyway, wore it like a cocoon, as if to protect myself from the crimes Father had long ago committed against me.

This sweater will become the one I'll wear when writing, day in, day out, year after year, until its cocoon transforms me. Transformed, I'll pupate in order to incubate words. My words will incubate, then pump their wings with bodily fluids until they, like the luna moth, become a swift, dressy creation that takes flight, *flight*.

"Thank you," I whisper. For a small moment in time, we're gifted by the gifts we've given and received. For a small moment, we aren't the victims of victims, but are deemed to become veritable kin because memory, concentrated as death, sleeps at the rock bottom of the Rock River. While memory, concentrated, deathly, sleeps at the rock bottom of the Rock River, love reigns supreme, brief as peace, but supreme.

XX.
GETTING THE BOY

Soon after, long after, I pack up everything I own in a sedan, half the size of a small house, move out to the very seacoast I'll return to when my long marriage fails. I move to the seacoast to be a Poet where I live in ratty apartments, take crappy jobs, date crappy men until I meet Scott. When I meet Scott, we fall in love, quickly, quietly.

After we fall in love, Scott moves into my ratty apartment. Weekday evenings find us playing cribbage on the rickety kitchen table. We talk and fall into grace as we move small pegs, like pale stars in a baleful constellation. We fall into grace, sense that sorrow, joy are two sides of the same coin. We mix them, like sugar peppered by salt. When we make love, we're salted by this peppery sweetness that's unheeded elsewhere. All of earth marries us, as does the Mary birds, the Mary night and the Mary Mother. Heaven lowers itself into our bodies, then stays, like mist which doesn't know how to weep.

Weekends, Scott and I go to get his boy, but not the baby, because he's too young. I like the boy best when he's asleep, after he gives me that funny little kiss at bedtime. I like him when moonlight glistens on the points of his eyelashes, when his face is composed of sorted, rare colors. I like him when he stands on the chair to help me make dinner, as he peers into the curve of Grandma's green bowl, which is deep enough for trees to take hold, where all we've ever dreamed of goes, even moonlight and disaster.

The boy asks for parsley, garlic. He asks me to be his best friend. When I say yes, we plunge our hands into the meatloaf, mix it up.

Scott and I live together all that winter, through sudden, startling snows, through winds which do more harm than good. Toward the end of March, we haul his motorcycle out of winter storage. It feels good to watch Scott hook up the battery, gas tank and fuel line again, as if we've made it through. I watch his foot come down hard on the starter, his body flying up, suspended, then coming down hard. The bike starts up with a sound like ice heaving apart.

He takes me for a short ride--the cold air rushes up my sleeves and the thick, mauve smell of the thaw riddles my bones. As we ride, the wind shoves between my ribs, cracking them open like doors. The ride ends. We've circled the block.

Scott pulls on layers of clothing for the long trip back. A leather smock laces up the sides, a blue jean jacket over the smock, torn gloves. On the way home, I follow him with the car, as I had done last October when we put the bike in winter storage. I drive in the radius of wind caused by him and the bike. I need to stay in his windfall, but other cars get in between us when he disappears over the top of a hill. Too easily, he disappears too soon from my life. He takes the boy with him, leaves an emptiness that ripples in circles, widening balefully.

When Scott disappears, taking the boy, our joy disappears, leaving sorrow on two sides of the same coin. It, too, widens balefully. The Mary birds, Mary night and Mother see my sorrow, protect me, as if with a caul. In this manner, I become a caul bearer again and remain one until I come to bear my own boy in glory, like a blessing that comes from the grave.

Now my boy is mostly grown, yet I've spent years getting the boy to bed, to daycare, to school. Years getting the boy to play dates, friends' houses, getting the boy to do his homework, getting his laundry done, breakfasts, lunches and dinners made, getting the boy clothes, getting him love--from me, his dad, family, friends, dogs, even buttercups--when suddenly, there's no boy to get.

Then I cry myself to sleep, clutching his teddy bear instead of hugging him. Not getting the boy is eerie, wrenching--it breaks my heart for years, is akin to painfully taking down a huge tree, twig by twig. Only the root ball stays intact, but that root ball is strong, neither bitter nor stunted. Nothing, no one can pull it, or me, from this earth. For this, I love the mom I am. More so, I love who I am.

Scott's boy is also grown. Now his other baby is grown, too, as are the children he had with his second wife, Bette. Still, it is with Scott and Scott alone that I'll wake the bones of my house, from its tubular bones to crow bones, port bones to Buddha bones, even the bones of Queen Elizabeth, dead for five hundred years.

With Scott, I'll wake the bones of my house and in rehabilitating it, rehabilitate me. Rehabilitated, no one will ever come to take me away again.

XXI.
SHEEP IN NEED OF A SHEPHERD

"Mom, Dad," I say, "this is Coriander, daughter of the Morgan mare, Amethyst." I hold out my hand, let Coriander's tongue, warm as mink, lick the salty crevices in my palm, then look at my parents who're hovering in the bulky, benevolent shadows of the mares. These shadows engulf their brittle ones.

I go over to Mother. She clings to her white pocketbook as though it were the Communion Missal Grandma gave me as a child. I lead her to Amethyst who lowers her gorgeous head in greeting. If I were to tell the mare to kneel before Mother, she would, even though this mare is regal.

"Touch her nose," I whisper, "it's warm, soft, like a petal with fur."

Mom's hand pulls back. Even the circuitry of her nerves retract into its black web.

"No," she murmurs, "I'm afraid." I want to tell her how I love the cathedral-like bones in Amethyst's skull, how they seem marbled with the music I perform, in line after poetic line.

"No need to be," I assure her, "these are gentle giants." As I say this, I think how Mom and Dad, who shrink in barn light, once loomed larger than the benevolent shadows of these mares, which engulf their own brittle ones. Back then, they were more severe than my Savage Maker, but now they're little more than cardboard figures in a toy theatre, a tragic one at that.

"What about you, Dad?" I ask, but he shakes his head *no* as if it were filled with the salts of time. Both parents step backward, rub against each other like charcoal drawings, shudder.

"Coriander is pregnant," I go on, "she's due to foal near Mother's Day." As I say this, I remember how studding this mare was the last act the mother of the two boys I now care for performed before she died in a car accident. She'd been run over by a sixteen wheeler.

I walk down to the end of the barn where Thyme, the big gelding, is twirling his bridle like the jokester he is. It's been about six months since I moved to the farm to care for Chad and Jamie, these horses, chickens, sheep.

"We're worried about you," Dad offers, "we're afraid you've taken on too much." He never asks about my writing, which is why I came out to the farm. Although I take care of the boys and animals, once the kids are off to school and the barn chores done, I can write in the one room house I get as pay, along with a hundred dollars a week and a cord of wood. My house was a butcher shop. Underneath pulleys and hooks, the white margins of my pages widen to meet the horizon of sky.

I toss off, "I love it here," then throw the barn doors open, like a gilt frame to a painting none of us can own. The fields below beckon, become a sheet of accidental music. Snow falls, dainty snow--each flake is a tiny, blue antique.

I brush my long hair over my shoulders. It's wild, tangled, like Amethyst's uncombed mane. I look back at Mother and Father as they shiver in the antique light shed by the blue snow. "Really," I go on, "I'm in my element."

"But," Dad says, "these children aren't your own."

"Chad and Jamie?" I reply, "they're good boys. They just miss their mom. I'm here to help them not miss her too much."

I twitch, remember how, earlier in the fall, I'd stood with the boys, down in the remains of their mother's churned-up garden. Backwashed by silver clouds, Chad juggled apples while Jamie collected the last zinnias to make a strange bouquet, like a jester's hat, spraying this way and that as he tumbles through another bright, desperate song. When their father, Arthur, opened the gate, Chad dropped his apples, balanced on one leg, like a small, unprotected crane. Jamie grabbed my leg, gasping, as his father tossed out their mother's ashes, as if to top-dress her sodden, forsaken beds. He then dumped out a bucket of stove ash, blending the body of a woman with dead hunks of fire. I reeled from the children's skeletal, magnificent cries--*Mommy, Mommy!*--which crossed the sky like lightning.

Down in the field, the mares, disturbed, filed the fence rails with their teeth, as though it were a harmonica. They keened along with the barn dog who howled, like a supplicant, beneath the old chestnut tree, which swayed in wind that had stripped it of its heavy skirts. The children scattered, like birds after gun shot, while Arthur toed the ash and wiped his hands on his pants, as if to clean them after an odious task. When I asked, "Why?" he scoffed back, "why not?"

Dad presses on, "What about Arthur? How about the father?"

"Harmless, absolutely harmless," I insist, even though that's not entirely true. Once, when helping the boys with the evening chores, I had to catch the mare, Sassy, for them, as she needed to be brought up to the barn at night because she kicked and bit the other mares during the feedings.

When I got to her, I knew enough to show Sassy the empty feed bucket before attempting to lead her to the barn. As we went up the hill, I jerked the horse into circles to slow her down. Sassy knocked the bucket with her head. We circled again.

She rammed me. I went flying, let go of the feed bucket, but held on to her lead, as if this mare, this dark, solid mass of flesh, was what held me to the earth. When I hit ground, I rolled over, lifted my head. Sassy was rearing. Her belly shone like a black welt while her hooves pawed the air. I released the lead. The mare took off.

Chad rushed over to help me. When I looked up, Arthur, who had just gotten home from work, was whipping Sassy. She was rearing in barn light and looked as though she were dancing in fire. Arthur held the lead, brought the whip across her flanks with his free hand. "Bitch!" he yelled, "bitch!" Brindled bits of blood flecked the air. Was he yelling at the horse, his dead wife, or me? Frightened, I put my arms around the boys, feared for us all.

That night, Arthur snuck over to my one-room house, the old butcher shop, and stood over my bed. I sat upright, jackknife in hand. Moonlight glinted on its blade, like a sneer. Arthur backed down, retreating to his rambling farmhouse where his motherless boys trundled in motherless dreams, ones that I sometimes shared even though my own mother now stood, cowering before me.

"Do you want to help with the evening feed?" I ask, as I open the grain bin. The horses nicker softly as I scoop out sticky grain that smells of molasses, trampled grapes.

"I need a drink," Mother flatly states.

Father chimes in, "we both need a drink. Right this minute."

"Soon," I say, "but I need to finish the barn chores first." Hooves thunk against the stall boards, like logs turning in a fire. I make my rounds, note how the barred windows in each stall look like those in medieval castles.

"Almost done," I pronounce, as I soundly thump Tarragon's rump. He's a small, randy stallion, has his own paddock so he can't get to the mares. I wish Arthur had a paddock, too.

"C'mon," I rally, "let's feed the sheep." My parents sheepishly follow me out into the winter night, which has just fallen, like an ermine dream. The rooster crows, heedless of the hour. The black barn dog howls.

"I'm scared," Mom says.

I know this is true. I know she lives in a perpetual state of fear. She's fragile, bird-like, the fossil of a bird with a dinosaur's bone in it. I can't help but want to guide her away from the fear she perpetuates. Dad's scared, too, his face hooded by the collective magnitude of the winter night.

We trudge through snow toward the pen where sheep huddle like soft, grey roses. I hear Mother's raspy breath, how it gasps, blindly. I long to feed her drops of air from an eyedropper, honeyed drops, as if to stop her from downing the tinctured liquor she consumes.

Dad doesn't sound much better. He huffs as he shuffles--this man whose footfall once frightened me into submission, now pads through snow, barely upright. The forces of destruction he once used upon me are destroying him. Both my parents are being destroyed, from within.

I listen, hear how their breaths barely scratch the air, am a student of the architecture of breath. I draw my own in deeply, as though I were a about to embark upon a baroque requiem, but the only requiem we hear is the baas of sheep.

We approach the pen. The falling snow is no longer dainty--it stings as though each flake were a tiny diamond bit. I feel how these diamond bits of snow are lacerating my parent's faces. Mother lets out a pig squeak, like mine as a child, and the sheep, huddled like moth balls, baa even louder, way too loud for just a bevy of hungry sheep.

Alarmed, I signal to my parents to stand still. They do, stock still. I circle the pen, come to a dead stop, fall to my knees. Here, in a welter of moonlight, is a newly deceased deer.

"Don't look," I say in a big voice to Mom and Dad, "just go back to the car and wait. I'll be there soon, get you your drinks."

"We want drinks. Now," Father demands.

"This is a sheep pen, not a barroom," I shout, "Go to the car."

When I glance back at them, they move slowly, painfully so, like two old hunchbacks. They do not leave tracks behind them.

I turn back to the deer whose blood-flowers pattern the intricately patterned snow as I surmise her crisis. How she got into the pen eludes me, but it's clear that she rammed herself to death against the fence posts trying to get back out. I understand, far too intimately, her frenzied fear, for my pen had been my kindercoffin, the Playhouse and beyond.

"Sheep," I whisper, "just sheep, not wolves in sheep's clothing." I gather her still warm body in my arms. "They're sheep, only ewes, and soon-to-be lambs." I sob, bury my face in her limp neck, realizing that for this deer, these sheep had, in fact, been wolves in sheep's clothing, but are no longer. Now they're merely sheep in need of a shepherd, just like my parents. Must I be the shepherd who guides them?

As I heft the deer in the uneasy chill, I want to breathe my breath--sweet as the molasses-smelling grain--into her, breathe her back to life with drops of honeyed air. Although I can't do so for her, or Mom and Dad, I can breathe life back into the Little Bits I was.

With the deer blanketed in my coat, I make the long trek back to the farmhouse to give her to Arthur, like a sacrificial offering. I then take my parents to a tavern, let them drink, pick at their food while I pick at mine. There's no talk between us, only their drunken slurs hanging in the opaque, interior air.

During midnight's blackest hour, Arthur strings up the deer in the breezeway between my house and his. He guts her, then puts her body parts into the deep freeze. Hasn't my memory gone into the deep freeze, too?

I listen to him whistle as he guts the deer while sitting up in bed, jack knife in hand, like the one Father used to score angel wings into me. Minutes glint like moonlight on its blade, minutes during which my parents trundle in deathly dreams in the old inn down the road.

They're in the deep freeze, too. I ache as I thaw, one body part at a time, even though it will be years before my memory thaws, because remembering is done in the blood

Four:

THE DREAM THAT WAS ONCE US

Boston and the Berkshires, 1990-2008

"Enchanted Cottage, Winter Night"

XXII.
IN THE DREAM THAT WAS ONCE US

It's unpleasant that Donald and I have had a beginning and an end. Unpleasant to feel the rift of the infinite cleave him, cleave me, to feel how the last snows flattened us as they fell into crass jewels. Unpleasant that I no longer stoke the old, black Vigilant wood stove in the cottage in the Berkshires. Unpleasant to know how an intense cold bellows in its belly, like frozen sweat, and that the mute fireflies inside have been muffled into ash. Unpleasant that Donald no longer touches me because his fingers have strayed away, like numb monks on a pilgrimage from which they'll never return.

What else is unpleasant in the dream that once was you and Donald?

That the vows to be there in sickness and health have been broken and that we've gone from walking, hand-in-hand, like two old sweethearts, on the old logging trails in the rolling hills we so loved, to not walking, not speaking. Unpleasant that our breath no longer works in sync, like two pumps drawing up the same clear water. Unpleasant when pins of freezing rain porcupine us and to feel how our Eden has iced over.

What remains pleasant in the dream that once was the two of you?

It remains pleasant when Donald brings me, for the first time, to Great Meadows. Pleasant when he turns into a bird dancer by performing a mating dance while promenading the promontory. Delightful, when he flaps his arms and legs as my body becomes mast to his arbor where fat blossoms sing like birds.

From atop the tower which we climb, as though it's a widow's walk, we listen to the call of the red-winged blackbirds toot in air cold as the first, not last frost, while ducks settle--specks of soft ash--on the water's glazed foreskin. We listen, not only to the red-winged blackbirds, but to chickadees, titmice and downy woodpeckers, which drill with mettle in the wormhole. We hear robins whose bellies are the color of foxgrapes. We are in azimuth.

Beyond us, the marsh is tented with heaps of cattails, broken like thin masts: we, too, are this delicate, will wed the brokenness, the straws, the masts while red-winged blackbirds, chickadees and goldfinches in yellow-black tuxedos striate the sky with their cries. We'll smell the wormhole, its bevy of rot, the heavy odors of molt, blood and loss.

What else will you wed?

We'll wed the white-throated sparrow's call rising in the floating world: *don't leave me by myself.* We'll wed, unwed, become the living, the dead, the living. Before we become the living, the dead, the living, our son will skirt my hips, here at Great Meadows to peer at a frog crouched in a shroud of water, splayed by the weight of the male who clasps her back, flattening his coldness against her. It's then I'll know what breeds here, bred me, Donald, Ryan. What breeds us breeds these damselflies who, driven by the blue power in their scant bodies, rise above the shallows where carp school, spawning a spill of black flicks--dark bursts urging us into being what we must.

Is there more pleasantness?

There's always more, always less--it's pleasant when Donald's kisses, light as peas, shower down upon me. Pleasant when sparks fly up the flue of the old black Vigilant until it turns cello-red while the wood sings as it burns, like martyrs joyous in their deaths. Pleasant to watch the sugars of snow blossom into gasping flowers, to listen to the music from Bali on the stereo and sigh while opening my legs for Donald. It's melodious to feel his fingers wander down to my slickness, to be full of eros, thick as paint before it dries, to gaze up at our cathedral rafters, ruddy as canyons.

In our loft, green lacewings adorn dusty corners, like crinkly bows. The windows across from the bed are tall envelopes ennobling the purple night, dense as priestly vestments. I'm transported to being back on the old logging trails while walking with Donald, trails which crisscross the long, rolling hills. I'm transported back to being beneath trees metamorphic with mystery whose black branches are turgid with bull's blood. Transported to the fallen hemlock leaves, red as rice, to not questioning, but following Donald's earthly allure, like a hunch.

What else do you do?

We walk under watery prisms of light, which bevel into clouds big as cows, clouds that low until the hills grow musky with evening chill. We walk by old sugar shacks, henhouses--de-flocked, eggless--feel the heft of the infinite, cross bridges over creeks without beginning, without end, step over barbed wire twisted into rusty crowns. We walk and bed on the trails. We bed on a pyre of moonlight, on the still lathers of snow. We bed into the deepness we'll firmly hold onto.

What happens after your walks?

I get the fire going while Donald pours beer into a frosty mug. Frosty mug in hand, he goes to sit down in his favorite wooden rocker.

"Come," he says, as he holds his hands out to me. I undress, drop lingerie, like the lacy bits of snow falling beyond the windows where an owl hoots, fitful and alive.

"Shriek owl," I say, as I climb onto Donald's lap to sit on the rocker with him. "I used straddle boys, just like this, on the swings down at Bloom School so we could neck." I blow a kiss, catch it in my hands, plant it on Donald's cheek before leaning into him to tongue his tongue, feel him rise. Soon he's inside me and the blue harmonics of loss mute into sentient silence. I grab onto the chair rails, let him in deeper, move with him.

Suddenly, there's a snap, followed by a crack--we crash down onto the floor.

"We broke the chair!" I exclaim, while untangling myself, "good job!"

"Oh, no," Donald lets out, "it's my favorite chair!"

"Not anymore," I say.

He smiles, "I guess it's time to load the stove."

"Guess so," I answer as I open the black stove door, "you first, as it was your Papa Bear chair."

Donald chucks in a few rails. I chuck in some more. The stove fires up: *red roar, blue applause.*

We soon replace that Papa Bear chair, buy a Mama Bear chair, add a Baby Bear chair when Ryan is born. Winters we circle the wood stove, like a posse, listen to that *red roar, blue applause,* while telling stories. Summers we line up the the chairs, biggest to littlest, in front of the sliding glass doors to watch fireflies move, like glowing hula hoops, in tall grasses above which bats snarf up bugs, like dark mites which are all mouth, no soul.

"I love the bats most," says Donald, in his Papa Bear chair.

"I love the fireflies best," I say, in my Mama Bear chair.

"Me loves bugs," says Ryan, in his Baby Bear chair, as we nod our heads in agreement, like co-conspirators, who master the craft love wildly manifests before it goes asunder.

What about now?

We're still co-conspirators, crafting love. We do so with Donald in his Papa Bear house, me in my Mama Bear house and Ryan in the high offices of his dorm room.

Still, it remains pleasant to love the hills we loved, hills where our indelible deepness exists as if creased in black velvet. Pleasant to see how those hills tent themselves in the water beyond my windows, to walk beneath my own trees whose lower branches have fallen, like feathers to ground, because beauty loves loss.

What else is pleasant?

It's pleasant to cross the Spruce Creek bridge--without beginning, without end--which leads to my house. Pleasant to continue to parent Ryan with Donald, even though the vows have been broken. Pleasant to love the three bridges, three states between us and lovely to love the loft I sleep in, even though it's not the loft we slept in. My windows, like our windows, are also tall envelopes, ennobling the purple night, dense as priestly vestments.

Lovely to let my gaze graze over the water, like the fields Donald and I once waded through in snow high as the low backs of ponies. Now those ponies are penumbra, halflit, quickened by the darkest wanderings. Lovely this riff-raff wind that's here and there, the tasseled stars, the same grasses whose nubile antennae screw upwards.

What do you still share?

We share a ruby-throated hummingbird, even though we don't share the same house. Her pulse throbs in us as she migrates between our houses and, like our story, comes back changed. She shifts from the bit of sweetness in Donald's left earlobe to the sweetness between my lower lips, flits from his garden in the hills to mine by the sea, skitters from the scarlet bee balm there to the scarlet bee balm here--each bloom strange as the pom-pons on a jester's hat as he tumbles through another bright, desperate song.

For her, we've divided our succulence, thick as custard, the succulence we once bathed in by candlelight in our sunken tub. There, white carpeting surrounded us like an ermine pelt. The candle flames nodded like lily-of-the-valley when jostled by even-tempered breezes. As we bathed, the hummingbird sipped at lobes of candlelight, then at our heat.

Charged by that heat, the hummingbird appears, disappears, reappears, wafting a hieroglyphic wave in air fragrant as the shadows in puddles dark as cloves. Charged by our heat, she's iridescent as flame, as she plunges into us headlong with the gravity of her slightness. She's the weave that rivers us, a flying grotto, nave, black paradise. Donald's pale hand cups the left side of her, my pale hand the right, like a parenthesis, that gently rocks her into the cusp of the dream which once was us.

What happens in the dream which once was the two of you?

I go back to Donald as we climb the Cobbles. It's our favorite hike--the last stretch of trail is akin to scrambling up a stony top hat. Once on top of that top hat, we view an expanse of three rolling states. It's hot. Mauve haze hangs over the valleys like tissue gauze. We eat apples and bread, gaze down at stores and houses small as those in a Lionel train set. I'm laughing, wearing a pink swimsuit, crumpled shorts. Donald has a tank top tied around his head to keep the sweat from stinging eyes which stare back at me with sexual wonder.

Happiness plays between us like the white-throated sparrow's poignant cry: *I am the one for you.* This is before we take our vows. This is before we know how much my illness will weight our marriage, like the rocks in Virginia Woolf's pockets when she waded into the river to drown. Up on the Cobbles, there is no illness, no stones in my pockets. Up on the Cobbles, we're simply buoyed by the breathlessness of our desire.

Buoyed by our desire, the stream far below us is thin as thread, a stream too shallow to drown in--all we want to drown in is the affable ineffability of love. We do. But, when the thread of our love breaks, who's the one who pulls, the one who holds on? Don't we both pull, hold on at the same time?

What does that thread still thread through?

That thread threads through Ryan, strong, tensile, flexible as the willfulness that keeps us alive. That thread pulls, holds our years together, each month, a prayer threaded into the common book of prayers. Our thread is in the horizon-line smudged into mauve tissue and in the summers I spent in the rolling hills with Ryan when he was a little boy.

It's even in our neighbor, Nelson Candy, who I chance upon one warm evening where he says, "Spied an old bear crossing the trail which divides the hayed fields today."

"A white nose like an old dog's," he insists, "me and the wife were out back hauling in strawberries." He then points toward the woods the old bear took refuge in, woods I'd walked in earlier that day, woods which like a vision never appear the same. Soft-dappled by summer light, I chill at the thought of encountering bear upon its deserted trails.

"Knocked down Johnny Sawyer's cow fence last week," Nelson adds.

"Must be the same bear whose claws left gouge marks under little Ryan's windows, the one I spied at Sweet Water Farm, stripping trees of winter apples," I say, but Nelson's onto other things--the property he care-takes is up for sale. He's muttering how the price is too high, how at seventy, it's tough for he and the wife not to know where they might be.

I turn to take my leave--there's supper to make, my boy to care for. By bedtime, I've forgotten the old bear, how he might lurch through jewelweed to the compost pile where I tossed peaches, top-dressed with mold and pears dimpled with decay, earlier in the day. I kiss Ryan goodnight, then cover him with the cowboy bedspread that covered his father as a boy. The background mountain ranges are faint, but the red shirt of the wrangler and the flowers on the cacti remain blood bright, even in the low glow of the nightlight. The horse the cowboy rides is a gray ghost--likewise, his kerchief and the face of the brown steer he's wrangled down to ground.

Lowell's remark about poetry--meat hooked from the living steer--comes to mind, but my pen feels more like a blade of grass I might lay, in inky darkness, upon the rock that forms the cornerstone of my garden.

In bed, I read soft words calcified upon the page. Moths congregate at the window screen, thrumming dust from skittish wings, as though it were a sleeping powder. I'm soon washed over by dream and drift through the hollows of space while my unconscious inflates, like a blow-up angel who redeems, compels, magnifies the soul in its sumptuous waste.

I dream the elephantine beauty of private experience. I dream, in fluent wonder, of the organs in my body, soft as fetal heads, of the old bear clawing me open as though I were a trench deep with the darkest honey. Drugged by sleep, I succumb to the bear when he lowers his maw to devour my womb's rich nimbus.

I wake, shuddering, as if back in the throes of childbirth, then stagger into Ryan's room where the windows, those books of moonlight, illumine the mysteries which fall, soft as unshod breezes, upon his sleeping face. No bear has been here, but I climb into bed anyway. My boy's head smells malty, like dead-headed flowers, just as it did the moment he was born--although the ancients say we have two souls, the physical spark and the dream wanderer, I birthed a third in that hospital room to ghost and guide my soft, romantic child.

I summon forth this trinity of souls--dense with sensuous presences, they move like nursemaids about the bed, sing, quietly, in delectable voices. Ryan rolls closer to me--a log on a fire--safe beneath the dream catcher he made to ensnare, in the bright abacus of its leather web, the stately and doomed spirit of the bear, as though it were the ruined side of ourselves, which in its hunger to be whole brutally guts the beautiful worth inside us.

The old bear does gut the beautiful worth inside Donald and I. He trenches our bodies by clawing out the darkest honey while we trundle in dreams until, twenty years later, I pack up everything I own in a sedan, brown as a cigar box, move into my Sea Cabin, set about waking its bones.

XXIII.
A CHILD IS BORN
7:07 p.m., December 9th, 1992

After we exchange the vows to be there in sickness and health, we move into the Newton house on 15 Debussy Circle, weekend in the Berkshires. In our new house, Donald and I tinker in order to wink our baby's first cells into being. We do a lot of tinkering in order to wink the baby's first cells into being. After one such bout, I run into the living room, buck-naked, go up into a headstand.

Donald follows me. While tying closed his plaid bathrobe, he asks, "Elizabeth, why are you doing a headstand right after we've had sex?"

"I have a hypothesis," I say while upside-down. My biologist husband is fond of hypotheses. He understands hypotheses better than he understands me.

"And what is your hypothesis?" he replies, "How can it possibly relate to your doing a headstand after we've had sex."

"Lack of imagination," I answer, "that's why I'm a poet and you're a scientist."

"Elizabeth." Donald's getting testy.

"Okay, okay," I say as I come down, "this is my hypothesis--by doing a headstand, I'm giving your sperm the fast lane to my egg."

"You're crazy," says my biologist husband. It's not the first time he's told me I'm crazy, nor will it be the last.

I may be crazy, but my hypothesis works. Nine months later, I'm in hard labor. We're at home and Donald's keeping track of the timing of my contractions on a legal pad.

"Here I go," I say while hanging onto the clothes washer. Unlike the furniture, it doesn't move no matter how hard I hang onto it. "Who's your favorite poet?" I ask.

"Elizabeth Kirschner," Donald responds, "now breathe."

I breathe. "How far apart are the contractions?"

"About two minutes."

"Do we have any cheesecake in the house?" I ask. The evening before, I'd refused to leave the B.C. English Department's Christmas party without eating cheesecake, even though my waters had just broken. Donald panicked.

"No, there isn't," he says.

"Too bad," I answer, "I'm dying for some cheesecake." I brace for another contraction, moan. "That was a big one. Maybe we better go to the hospital now."

Donald jumps into action. He grabs my long-packed, old black Woolworth's bag and out the door we go.

"Geez-Louise," I declare, "it's cold!"

"I know," he replies, "but at least I got the car washed today."

This seems like a non sequitur to me until Donald tries to open the passenger-side door for me. It's frozen shut.

He runs around the car, as in a Chinese fire drill, gets in, goes onto his back, crab-like, pounds the passenger-side door with both feet, panicked once again.

I simply walk around the car, slip into the second seat behind my frenzied husband, then say, "We can go now."

Donald pops up, shocked. "How the?" he starts.

"It's okay," I interrupt, "just drive."

Ten minutes later, we arrive at Beth Israel hospital where I'm wheeled into a birthing room. Here I feel pressure, as though under the sea's tonnage. I'm culturing a pearl, or am the pearl being cultured, crushed and cultured. The pressure is the pain. It's also the pressure of the cold snow beating against the hospital window, darkly beating with the sound of whips, their clean leathery smell.

The pain wallops me until my ribs buckle, like those in a barrel, the hoops wrenching under old screws driven in too deep. These screws are being driven into me until my three D vision becomes four D. It's as though Dali were rioting in my mind--what I see are melting gloves, verdant fire, shadows lean as wands. Not a trace of baby scent anywhere, only the dire smell of blood as it ponders its arrival, blood tinctured by the oil that greases my uterine machine.

Pain walls me in. I grip Donald's hand, hard.

"He's a plant, not an animal," whispers my biologist husband.

I smile. All along, I've insisted that I'm carrying a plant, not an animal, but my biologist husband refused to believe me.

"Big root ball," he continues, as he pats my belly. I smile again, brief as peace, before pain walls me in once more. My body grows four sides, is a box my flesh is shrinking into it until an iron lid, shuts off my vision. With it goes the hospital room, its cantaloupe walls, the bed on its ferris wheels.

This powers me up. Powered up, the pain, smelling of old cellos and dank, animal musk torques into a fugue, which fluted, wild, geysers out of my head until what I'm birthing when I remember I'm birthing is not my baby, but baby Bach.

I'm certain I'm birthing Bach as birthing Bach invades my consciousness, which is little more than a dimpled hint in time. This dimpled hint means it's time to birth baby Bach.

"Bach," I cry into the stereo of Donald's palm as that palm is the only place my pain can go, "I'm birthing Bach." Chords are resounding, heavy as oars in oar locks, chords pound in my organs and my womb is an organ of muscular grace--it's a wet zither warbling the zenith of my pain. "Bach," I yell, "prepare the way for Bach!"

Donald is scared, really scared, yet I'm not. The specks in his eyes go fishing in Petri dishes while my pain continues its operatic rampage. "Bach," I repeat while pressing into a birth squat, "can't you hear him crown?"

Donald is saying, *you're crazy*. I dimly wonder if his telling me I'm crazy is exactly what will make me go crazy, but I'm too busy ripping off my Jolly Green Giant hospital johnny tied at my throat like a bib. A Green Giantess, I go up onto the bed with ferris wheels. Nurses appear, my Ob Gyn. I push, push harder, even shit a bit. My shit is whisked away as I push, then push some more.

The lights in the room are dimmed and the nurses swish around me, like ballerinas in sneakers. In between pushing, I doze. "She's dying," cries Donald, "can't you see she's dying?" but I rouse, push, rouse, push. After two hours, Bach comes barreling down my birth canal as though it were a luge. Are the walls of my birth canal icy? Will Bach come out blue with the cold? Will baby Bach be blue and I, bluely baroque? Birth is baroque, an intense fugue that ends in a catastrophic miracle. Slick as a fish, baby Bach slides out, is whisked onto my chest. It's 7:07 p.m.

When I smell the peach fuzz on baby Bach's head, how it's malty, like deadheaded flowers, I know that my baby isn't Bach. Still, he has arrived with no less genius than Bach. When my nipple, hard as a tuber, warbles into his mouth and Donald cuts the cord, the music doesn't stop. Organs groan in my organs. The hospital room, generic as God, is but a small cathedral where complex gongs ache in its steeple. My placenta gushes out.

Donald holds up the placenta, like a purple saddle bag, or a strange purse that he admires more than the baby at my breast. He's a biologist, after all. If there were a microscope in the room, the placenta would go under it. Donald wouldn't hear me cry, "No, no, no," when the nurses, as if in an evil fairytale, snatch my baby, my best magic bean ever, from my breast.

"He needs tests," they insist, but how can a baby, my best magic bean, need anything beyond my warbling nipple?

"Thieves!" I cry, as he's snatched away. Suddenly, my organs cease their organ music. Bach returns to the dead. I'm isolated, an animal stripped of its hide; musky, dank. My body, newly devoid of what it has carried so long is appalling, like a bruise on top of a lewd tattoo. If a bruise could agonize, mine does.

I'm reeled out of the birthing room into another one on the maternity ward where I lapse, briefly, into fitful sleep. When I awaken in the middle of the night, no baby in my arms, I panic, push the nurse button, hard.

"My baby," I shout, "bring him to me now!"

My now is a commanding one and that baby is in my arms in no time. "How dare you take him away from me," I snarl as the nurse bows her way out of the room as if before a Zen master.

I'm no Zen master, but my best magic bean is a Zen baby--at birth and in the days, then weeks that follow, I feel a mysticism nearly steam from my blessed, adorable little Ryan. It's there in the wee elephant ears of his shoulder blades, in the warm, velvet-like fontanel, in toes curled like the crabbed, cranial blossoms of Queen Anne's Lace. In my blessed baby, I see an almost deplorable sweetness, a sweetness boiled down into a milky essence, which is heady as the scent of a quivering foal in blood-brindled straw. I see his otherworldliness, how it emanates like mist from the slow moon of his face.

My little Ryan will transit with his otherworldliness until about three months old. Before then, Mom and Dad come out for a visit. As soon as they walk through the door, Dad sets up the leather satchel that is their portable bar. He fixes Manhattans, inspects his new grandson, then starts talking to Donald, as though my new child and I were extraneous.

Mom gawks at the baby with a frightened, feral longing, but when I hold him out to her, she lights a cigarette. I back off. As she pulls on her cigarette, my papery insides glow. Are bones from my body missing, adrift in the dark scene of her?

Next morning, when I go into the bathroom, I notice that Mom's old, cracked cosmetic bag is open. It's next to the salmon-colored sink. When I peer in, I see a vial of holy water, a rumpled piece of paper with the priest's instructions on how to baptize little Ryan.

Mom knows we have no desire to baptize the baby--Donald's Jewish, I a non-practicing Catholic. My boy came into this world without sin, original or otherwise. All babies do--it's we who transgress against them.

The holy water goes down the toilet, is flushed away. I crumple up the piece of paper, slam-dunk it in the trash. I don't say a word to Mom about her plans to baptize Ryan behind my back, but it is he who will announce, at age four, his spiritual leanings. "I'm a pagan," he declares, from the back seat of the car.

"A what?" Donald and I ask in unison.

"A pagan," he pipes in, again. His tone let's us know that the subject is now closed. My Pagan baby will become a Pagan boy, then a young Pagan man--not dark in the darkest manly sense, but bright in the bright world that is his, mine, ours.

XXIV.
IN COLD SPRING PARK

Soon after, long after, Ryan's birth, Donald and I go out on a date. After dinner, we drive to Cold Spring Park. January has stepped into the rooming houses of the poor, their cold parlors, unlit hearths, which are cathedrals for the dispossessed. I wonder if the sky is one such cathedral, or a box of diminuendos, as I move my lips in prayer. I pray, silently, asking for the blessing of a kiss, just one kiss to be bestowed upon me by my husband.

The wind, like an insurgent, charges in. Since the baby's birth, and in the years to come, such evenings are and will remain rare--a gold coin we're afraid to touch, let alone pass between us. We're letting the distance between us grow, as though the sadness of geography were keeping us separate, even though we're only a few inches apart. A diminuendo rains down from the ebony-rose sky; frankly melodic. The moon, a seed pod, swells with spore-filled milkweed froth while the trees assume melancholy stances, crowned by empty nests ruffled with last autumn's burnished leaves.

We're parked on a circular drive in Cold Spring Park. The circular drive goes round a towering oak, much like the one outside my bedroom window in the old Rockford house.

It's a grandiose oak with many wounds. The wounds are black as the ebony-rose night. I want to wrap gauze around them, dress them up. Instead, shreds of toilet paper cling to the lower branches, like the underthings of fallen angels.

I, too, feel fallen, surely no angel, but a woman who's falling from lesser grace to no grace in her husband's eyes. Over the years, I do fall, then fall more, bouncing like a ball down the cellar stairs.

In my heart, there resounds another diminuendo--it feels permanent, as if dyed in oxblood while Donald and I sit in the car, silent as the prayer I mouth. We stare at the ground surrounding the grand oak. Long white feathers, hundreds of long, white feathers have been stuck into the earth. Who, I wonder, painstakingly planted them, one by one? Shouldn't we all plant feathers as talismans of who we might become?

I reach over, touch one of Donald's hands, which are at ten and two on the steering wheel, like the hands of a clock. The hands on my clock are also frozen at ten and two. Ten and two, two and ten--in between, a girl in an icy chrysalis, who dreams to eclose in a vernal, vaunted dawning. Until then, she sleeps in her chrysalis, a sleep as concentrated as death.

When I reach across the distance that keeps the distance between us and touch Donald, he doesn't flinch. Hasn't he learned how to share me with our baby son? Will he ever? Or does he fear the baby and I are enclosed by a mystic circle he can't step into? Aren't Donald and I becoming artful at vocalizing silence amid the melodic diminuendos when it would be more fruitful to vocalize our needs?

That we cannot, do not, will not vocalize our needs will artlessly wound us. It will also wound the towering oak that is our marriage. We just don't know it yet. We don't know how this not-knowing, this absolute refusal to speak is wounding us and our marriage. In the end, our refusal to speak will cast us all out of the mystic circle.

For now, Donald sits, mesmerized by that island of feathers, the one I can't sail around to reach him. I'm unable to sail around it because I'm anchored beside him. Anchored, I long to kiss my husband, to caress his cheeks, their high, cool bones. I long to be kissed, caressed back, so much so, I again reach across the distance that keeps distance apart, try to draw him near, but he keeps his hands on the steering wheel, doesn't glance my way.

Suddenly, I'm pierced by the long, elegant bones of these hundreds upon hundreds of feathers. They fly like ivory arrows into my Sebastian heart--I may be no angel, am but a poor sinner--aren't we all?--here in the cold parlors of January. No fire roars in the cathedral of its hearth--only the ashes murmur, ashes soft as the feathers, many feathers.

But their lean bones go right through me--this piercing silences me. Pierced, I again ponder the one who planted these feathers around the lonely oak, this tree of wounds, mortal wounds.

A thought flies into my brain: even with all these lordly feathers on this patch of earth, the island can't fly. Not only can this island not fly, I, too, am forbidden to fly by the one who has sentenced me to be so anchored I can't sail across the distance between Donald and I. This island, here in Cold Spring Park, is far from the pillow islands Ryan and I will place between the beds to leap from--it's an island of near violent isolation, the one the guillotine will *whoosh* through, years later, when we're in Bequia.

I finger my wedding ring--it has the tree of life etched in it. I'm also wearing a dress with a coral tree of life silk-screened on to the front panel. Does this make me a tree of many wounds which gape open, each a black paradise, or living gargoyle?

I don't know, so I start making wild bird noises; they up-flutter on my lips. Donald remains quiet, as his distaste for my emotional displays grows. He turns the car on, drives home while bird noises up-flutter on my lips.

Once at home, I go into the nursery while remembering a line of poetry about wild birds in the aviary of the mind. Mine needs sanctuary--I find it in Ryan's room with its spongy undergrowth, plural presences flocking around the crib.

I quietly close the door, release the long shush of a breath. Here, in the blue light shed by the nightlight, lies my sleeping son. His hands, soft as peaches, are cupped around his ears, intent on listening to who he might become. Plural presences, his bevy of angels, flock around the crib. Wing palpitations match his heart's--there's a soft shuffling of bare feet, a courtly dance to court him--all infants are of royalty, even if they don't come from it. I bend over, scoop him up, go to the rocking chair where love tips into fear and back again.

His candled warmth infuses me while I begin to sing. I sing to Ryan, as we gently rock. This moment, like so many with him, is a piece of peace on a silent night. He is my refuge, I, his safe harbor--with him alone, I sail while anchored. My soul, adorned with all those lordly feathers, takes *flight,* as does my baby boy's. We make a little music as we move in *flight.* I'm moved by it. No one, no one else at all can hear this music, but it is the music we're meant to perform.

I stay in Ryan's room all night. As dawn ecloses on rosy hinges, he opens his eyes, smiles his prescient smile. I nurse him, remember how, when he was a newborn, his eyes would roll up into his head, as though he were drunk on breast milk. I sing some more to him--together we return from the shores of lullaby. I look at his eyelashes, long and sweeping, wonder how often his lids will open, close upon a world, emboldened by the darkest manly sense.

Over breakfast, Donald's eyes are vacant, a room he walked out of long ago. My own eyes open, close, open upon our marriage, see how it's becoming darkened by the darkest manly sense. My husband wordlessly picks up the paper--he does this every morning. Anything but a firm denial that our marriage is being darkened, would be an affront to his dignity. My silence, constructed out of the fear to speak my fears, only upholds his need to formally confirm that, in his eyes, I'm falling from lesser grace to no grace, as is our marriage.

It will take days to warm Donald up again. After our visit to Cold Spring Park, he'll sleep in the basement on more nights than I can count. The conjugal bed where we tinkered Ryan's cells into being, will become another flightless island around which I'll try to sail to reach my husband, but there among the silence of feathers, I'll remain silent, reprimanded by Donald's absences.

Anchored on the marital bed, my lament rises: *Pray tell, love, why do I remember the bones of a bird I once found in a crown of dead leaves flecked by early frost, how when I brought it to you, cupped in the nest of my hands, all I wanted to do was wake its bones, bones that are ash, char, ash?*

XXV.
DAD GOES TO THE OTHER SIDE

Soon after Ryan's first holidays--we spend them as a family at Marie's--Dad goes off the road in a blackout. The doctors say more blood needs to be going into his brain, so into the hospital he goes for routine surgery to open up his carotids. While recovering, he asks Mom to smuggle in booze for him. Good Catholic that she is, she goes to the hospital's chapel to ask God if she should smuggle in the booze. God says, *Yes,* in a big voice. She sneaks in a flask hidden in a brown paper bag. Dad chugs it down.

When home from the hospital, he chugs down more booze, smokes, too. He falls into a coma, goes back into the hospital, comes around, is sent back home where he drinks, smokes. On Superbowl Sunday, Dad falls into a coma again, returns to the hospital, but doesn't come around, so he's put on a vent in Neuro-Intensive Care. His room is a fish bowl so he can be observed at all times, like an animal in a tank.

January passes into February. Dad remains in his coma. Gene calls with daily reports. Every time the phone rings, I cringe. Every time I pick it up, I expect him to say, "Dad's gone." Although he was a cruel father to the Little Bits I once was, his pending death feels gothic.

Night after night, when the phone rings, often after midnight, Donald grabs it, rolls over, passes it to me.

"Gene?" I ask, even though I know it's him. On this particular night, the metallic snow skitters against our picture windows, sounding like Komodo dragon scales. Thousands of dragon scales.

"We almost lost him," says Gene. There's a hundred years of weariness in his voice. "His feet turned black."

"Oh my God," I whisper. I hear nurses swishing around in the background, like ballerinas in sneakers.

"He was dying from the feet up," he continues. "I just grabbed them, said, 'No, you can't go. Not yet."

"And?"

"He didn't go. His feet went from black to blue. They throbbed."

"Okay, hang in there." More Komodo dragon scales skitter against the picture windows.

"It's snowing," I say, as if talking about the weather could stop Dad from dying.

"Oh," Gene says, "it's snowing here, too."

"Probably the same flakes. A helluva lot of flakes, like fish food."

"A ton of fish food. We're getting buried."

"So are we," I say. I want to add that at least Dad isn't, at least not yet, but maybe that's bad luck.

"Night," Gene says, with another hundred years of weariness in his voice.

"Night," I say. My voice is just as weary. That makes a lot of years of weariness, too many to count.

February passes into March before Donald, the baby and I can go see Dad. Because we both teach at Boston College, we have to wait until Spring Break. The day finally arrives for us to go.

We wake to snow copulating with more snow. It comes down dreamily, like the insides of the Milky Way. Ryan now goes to day care, which is kiddy-corner from our house. I usually take him, but on this cold, snowy morning, Donald offers. I agree--it will give me more time to pack.

Minutes later, the phone rings. "Gene?" I ask, "is it you?"

"No," comes the reply, "it's Auntie." She's the Indonesian woman who runs the day care.

"Why are you calling, Auntie? Donald's bringing the baby over."

"I have the baby," she says, "he's fine."

"Then why are you calling?"

"It's Donald," she says, quietly.

"What about him?" I ask.

"He never made it to the door."

"What do you mean he never made it to the door? How can you have the baby if Donald never made it to the door?" I'm confused, alarmed.

"I saw him cross the street."

"And?"

"I've called 911."

"What do you mean you've called 911?" My voice is rising.

"When Donald didn't come to the front door after crossing the street, I went out. He fell on the ice, Elizabeth. You need to come over here."

I hang up, grab my parka, run out in my slippers, cross the street, find my husband still sprawled where he went down.

"Donald!" I cry, as I go down on my knees. His ankle is angled, like a flag at half mast, his shoulder dislocated. He's down for the count.

Neighbors gather. They bring blankets. Over and over, they say, "He saved the baby. It's a classic save-the-baby story."

"He's in shock," I declare. "Where the hell is the ambulance?" I'm panicked. Donald may have saved the baby, but who's going to save him? Snow is still copulating with more snow. The insides of the Milky Way continue to fall, blindingly.

I hear sirens in the distance. They stay in the distance. "Christ," I say, "why isn't the ambulance here?"

Snow keeps birthing. The cold's chaffing Donald's cheeks while his eyes dull, like the thick green glass in old coke bottles. We wait for the ambulance to come. We wait some more for the ambulance to come. Minutes heap upon minutes while the snow copulates. It's sticking to my husband's blue lips. I bend over, kiss it away. His dull eyes blink, as if to say, "thank you." When the ambulance finally comes, we find out it couldn't get up the hill we live on because of the snow.

The EMTs load Donald up. I follow the ambulance to the hospital, stay within its windfall. He's rushed into the ER where a fleet of doctors and nurses pounce on him. After a shot of morphine, X-rays are taken and he's whooshed into surgery, only to come out with nine pins in his ankle.

He's really down for the count. The doctors tell me he'll need much care, be on crutches for two months. I call Mother from the hospital.

"Mom," I begin. My voice is shaking as though a baby rattle's in it. "I have bad news." She croaks a frog sound over the phone, says, "I don't want your bad news. When are you going to be here?"

"Well," I go on, "that's the bad news."

"What the hell do you mean?"

"Donald fell on the ice this morning. He broke his ankle in three places, dislocated his shoulder."

"Too bad, but when are you going to be here? I need you."

"I'm sorry, I can't come. I have to take care of my husband."

"I don't believe you," Mom declares. She's hornet-mad.

"Please, please understand. I can't leave him."

Mom pauses. "How dare you do this to me?"

I just say, "love you."

"Like crap you do." She doesn't know what else to say. As she hangs up on me, I whisper, "Give my love to Dad."

Days pass, a delirium of days while I take care of my husband, who's in great pain. I also take care of the baby, continue teaching. When Donald's finally able to hobble around by himself, spring has descended with its unanimous green theme. Trees are pimpled with buds coated with baby hair. Red shoots press up from black dirt, like soft periscopes.

I finally take Ryan to go see Dad, who's becoming undone, creating death, his only masterpiece. The flight is long, my now toddling infant so active, a flight attendant yells at me to keep him still. I look at her helplessly, say "My father is dying." She turns away.

As soon as we get to Rockford, Gene takes us out to the hospital and into the fish tank room where I wash my hands and the baby's. The television is on, Dad propped up in bed, as if he could watch it.

A golf match is being aired. Perfect! Dad loves golf! He can't move, can't speak. His hair's uncut, wavy, his toenails so long they could be hooves. I carry little Ryan over to the bed.

"Dad," I whisper, "here's your grandson. He's traveled a long way to see you."

He can't respond, but his face clarifies, like butter. "Your grandson wishes you could hold him."

After a moment of silent heart-speak, Ryan points his index finger at what remains of his grandfather, who's become lean, elegant, even in a hospital johnny. Then it happens--Dad slowly, barely, lifts his index finger. Little Ryan touches it with his. It's an E.T. moment. Gene and I, let go, sigh.

*   *   *

When Dad finally does come out of his coma after four long months, he's brain-damaged, out of it for good. Out of it, he's put into a nursing home, just like Grandma.

I journey to see him one more time. Gene takes me to the nursing home, which reeks of sweat, piss. Dad drools--his spit's full of seed I want to plant with my touch. Gene carefully rigs him up to a portable oxygen tank, reels his wheelchair outside into light bold enough to blare. Dad, the old malcontent, looks content. It's as though his dirty dish rag soul were being cleansed. Behind the azure sky, not just the stars, but our stars align themselves while grass preens itself green.

"Love," he spells out on his spelling board, "love!"

"A perfect one word poem," I spell back. Dad smiles.

Mom shows up, lights a cigarette, blasts smoke at him, says, "he's not my Bill." Gene and I look on, shocked, as miserly smoke wreaths his face.

"Mom," I start.

Gene picks up, "Mom, maybe it's not such a good idea to smoke around Dad since he can't breathe on his own. Could you please put out your cigarette?"

"You're ganging up on me," she replies, belligerently, as she drops her butt, leaves.

We reel Father out of the blare of light, back into the hall where the nearly dead hold court with no one but themselves.

Dad doesn't remember our names, but that night he yanks out his breathing tube, gets up, no, falls out of bed, to run away with his high school sweetheart, Suzy.

Next day, he calls me his Suzy. He's all smiles. His eyes are misty, as if perfumed by a peach dawn. As I tuck him into his nursing home bed, his thin, white sheets are stiff as the ice-turreted dirt in my garden when I put it to bed each autumn. Dad's head sinks into a pillow, blonde as Hosta leaves when their thin, albino-white blood's been drained by November's clear austerities. I suspect Dad's blood is just as thin and albino-white.

"Dad," I begin, "are you there?"

He blinks once, as if to signal 'yes' the way I'll do when in a paralytic seizure. One blink, yes, two blinks, no.

"That's a pididdle," I remark. "It's a game Jack Sparks and I used to play in high school. If I saw one headlight missing in a car, I'd cry out, *Pididdle,* and was awarded a kiss. Two missing headlights was a Pidaddle, which was worth two kisses."

Dad blinks again.

"Pididdle," I cry, "you get a kiss!" I bend over, place my cool lips on his forehead.

Dad blinks twice.

"Pidaddle," I exclaim, "good job!" I then place two kisses on his eggshell-thin forehead.

Will it break open? Bloom? Does the flame of his dark love loiter somewhere in his body? Perhaps in his toes, bulbous nose, purple hands? I start to pat him down, searching for that heat.

"Hot beans," I say, "Hot beans! Here in your left wrist, your hot spot's pulsing like a firefly."

I take his ET finger, place it on the spot in his left wrist. For a moment, the flame of his dark love ignites--his face becomes as transparent as November's clear austerities, regal barrenness. For a moment, I finger-rake his hair, like the crowns of the cut-back perennials in my garden, then glance out the single, curtain-less window. Beyond, there's a sad, Midwestern sun filled with coarse salt, bones, milk dust.

"Dad," I start up, "how about one last round of 'Little Rabbit Foo-Foo?" It's his favorite game now.

His bunny ear fingers go up, like a peace sign. I sing for him as his bunny finger ears go, *hop-hop.*

"Little Rabbit Foo-Foo goes hopping in the forest," I belt out the words like a smoky torch singer, but see myself in my garden dragging rafts of leaves, cool as scalps, into the woods on a blue tarp. The woods, banked in decay, smell beery, like Dad's breath.

"Down comes the fairy godmother." Dad looks eager for me to be the fairy godmother, but I'm that gardener flipping her tarp, like a boat. Leaves, debris and the ache of passed-out blooms scatter around, high as down, which snow after snow will pack down until the huge, ungodly blooms are pressed into a winey residue.

Just like Dad. I have sung the whole song. I'd sing some more, but Dad looks sleepy, small, like a troll lost in a fairytale and we all know that not every fairytale has a happy ending.

I stand in the doorway a moment while Dad passes, a passed-out bloom into one of his last sleeps before permanent sleep. While in the doorway, I'm also standing in the empty dressing rooms of my garden. In the lean elegance of things stripped down at eventide, I'm standing in the clear austerities, regal barrenness. His life. My life. All life.

Coarse salt, bones, milk-dust. Only in the Midwest can the sun look sad. As I leave my father in the nursing home, I leave the coarse salt bones crave, the milk inside them, their dust.

* * *

As summer shallows out of its unstoppable growth, I work in the garden where, one day, little Ryan discovers a bird skull. He touches the eye holes where vision had flared out, brings it to me. It's paper stiff, soft enough to crush, a miniature O'Keefe. I slip the skull onto my fingertip--a finger puppet! My boy laughs, claps his hands. How can I not want to create, fashion, form the entire bird for him, I who am filled with scraps of melodious emptiness?

That night I dream of a soprano singing the "Ave Maria" in a church choir loft. Her gorgeous voice reverberates in my cheekbones. There's a dreadful affirmation in that voice--I feel permanently welded to it, as if to the insides of a Bach chorale.

Dad dies at dawn. It's the end of August. He dies while a nun quietly prays over him. He needs those prayers. And many more. That he trespassed against me is an understatement I'll live with for the rest of my life, but that he remains unforgiven is the truth I live by. I'm not sure he is forgivable, but I can let him--and Mom, rest. It's enough.

At Dad's funeral, I help my young son place a white rose on his coffin, then nurse him to keep him quiet. A soprano starts to sing up in the choral rafter. As in my dream, she's singing the Ave Maria. Her voice inspires another dreadful affirmation. My shining cheekbones ache. I'm inside that Bach chorale, want to cry out, *Bach, Bach,* while feeling how this soprano's voice is nothing but an excruciating beauty. What is beauty if it isn't excruciating?

At the moment when the priest turns the Host and the wine into the body and blood of Christ, in the midst of this holy moly moment, my child pops off my nipple, says, in a big voice, "Other side." Marie and I, though weeping, laugh--a ripple goes through the entire congregation. Although Father has made to the Other Side, I don't yet know that I, too, will make it to the Other Side, only I won't have to die to get there.

XXVI.
ELIZABETH AMONG THE LOWEST OF THE LOWLY

Soon after, long after Dad goes to the other side, the seizures start. The seizures start at the end of Ryan's kindergarten year. When they do, they go on for years, jinxing my brain, in seizure after seizure, with a weird, cruel wizardry. While my brain is jinxed by that cruel wizardry, I'm among the lowest of the lowly in room after hospital room. These hospital rooms have no forest in them, no evergreen air. They're sealed, like ziplock bags filled with formaldehyde. The formaldehyde preserves, but doesn't cure. Hospital rooms preserve, do not cure.

In them, I'm punctured for the drip-drip of IVs until my veins become scarred. Scores of tests are taken, fill my chart like a tome, to which is added a drawing Ryan makes of my jinxed brain. In the drawing, it looks like there's a bunch of bugs scurrying around in the tunnels of my brain, like the rubbery creepy crawlers I made as a child with my creepy crawler set.

Sometimes I can feel those creepy crawlers scurrying in my jinxed brain tunnels. Sometimes, they scratch their rubbery heads with their thin, rubbery legs, wondering what they're doing in my brain tunnels. My brain is given jinxed brain food--med after med after med. *Gobble-gobble, gobble-gobble.*

In one room, I wear a headdress of EEG leads, like an exotic, electrified green bird, for five days, five nights. For five days, five nights, I can only move from the bed to the bathroom in my bird headdress. In another room, I'm left lying on a bedpan overbrimming with my own pee for over an hour--peeing on the bee may be fun, but lying in my own isn't. In still another room, I wake in the middle of the night in the ICU with a breathing tube shoved down my throat. I also wake to two black eyes--I'd fallen down concrete steps into a concussion, then a seizure. In the ER, they cut off my clothes, gave me a shot to paralyze me in order to perform an MRI, after which they put in the breathing tube.

In another hospital room, I tend to my roommate--blind, confused--who screams for the nurse because she's unable to find the call button. I place the foam slippers with smiley faces on her feet, adjust her blankets, then pad back to bed hugging my son's favorite bear, Gund, through seizure after seizure. On the floors, above and below me, body after body gives up its life. A child is born dead. So are stones--yet we hold them in our hands.

In an odd revery, my IVs become the tap lines strung from our trees up in hills when puckered with late snow. The purple and teal tap lines are strung, like Chinese jump ropes. I don't know why or how the sap runs, just that it does. The lines bleed the clear light. The clear light bleeds me with the soft sugars of grief. Drops of it roll down my body like cum. Slow as spring. As mercy when we ask for it.

Outside the hospital window--grey day, grey night. Even so, my green-glorious dreams are impregnated by the storms that pitch in my jinxed brain. I know the star charts are coming and my soul will be wrapped in one, hushed, aglow. I know Kirschnerian Kyries begin in the ER--move on from there. I dream my brain is algae rising like bursts of yeast on a summer pond, algae I wet my hands in, sliding aside its shimmering curtain to watch drowsy salamanders. Has each slipped from my womb tasting of sunrise?

When I tell the neurologists how the bower bird loves blue and the tree toad has gold gilt, like ancient kohl, around its eyes, they sadly shake their heads, prescribe more meds, leave me to tremble alive, dead, alive. The hours, long as the stretcher I'm stretchered in, stretch into years during which I tremble alive, dead, alive again.

I, along with the other patients and nurses, are ants in an ant farm, working industrially for that unattainable state of health we're all dying for. We work hard to be well--shove the breath out, suck it in. Over and over, the blood pressure cuff tightens, expands, like a cervix giving birth while l long to give birth again, knowing that the birth I long to bring forth is my own elusive life.

Outside my window, seagulls, many seagulls. These seagulls have been tossed into a blanched sky, like a magician's hankies, or hundreds of communion gloves. How could I've known then that they'd become my white saviors? Could it be the gulls' fickle attitude toward altitude, their flight pattern of fragmented grace, or is that they, too, are among the lowest of the lowly, even if they see earth from a high point of view?

No matter that it will take years for these saviors to save me, it only matters that they do. Until then, there'll be many seizures, sometimes multiple in a single day. I'll have seizures on playgrounds, in elevators, grocery stores, on street corners. Most leave me flailing, others paralyzed.

My seizures not only debilitate me, they affect Donald, Ryan, too. Even if they don't flail, or are paralyzed, a part of them goes down when I do: heartbreak is democratic--mine breaks, theirs breaks--until I rise once more as Plath's Lady Lazarus: *fall down ten times, get up eleven.*

Some seizures leave me feeling as though I've been bitten by a black spider. This black spider is not the itsy-bitsy spider, but one whose venom paralyzes me. A spider no bigger than my fingernail. This is when I feel the sky's migrations. I feel night coming on, listen to it. Only my eyes blink, rooted in a language all their own--one blink, yes, two blinks, no.

I long to spell simple needs with my breath--*bathroom, water*--as if it were possible for these wishes to be fulfilled. Donald presses a hand on my forehead, as if to take my temperature. Ryan brings me pillows, ready to build a fort around me.

When he plays classical guitar, Donald drops tips into his open case, as though our son were a musician in a subway station. They both know my heart's clapping, despite the black spider's bite.

After one such bite, I rise, am Lady Lazarus, watch Ryan as he spies a magnolia warbler. Sky-sprung, this magnolia warbler lands on our doorstep, dropping like a blossom suckled by song. Sun-yellow underside streaked with black--has she, too, been charred with scar?

Ryan approaches her on tiptoe--all his young life, he's longed to pet a wild bird. She doesn't move when his fingers brush the blown light of her feathers, nor do I. Boy and bird--inside the black diamond of her eye, he grasps a twigged being vibrating within.

Flying in and out of the house, Ryan sets down a bowl of milk, as if for a lost kitten, but we we're the lost ones. Our lostness is alleviated by her quizzical visit--the yellow tears of light bibbing her breast smear away, for the moment, the black aura of my seizures, which seize mother from son.

Whistling through the space made by my boy's missing front teeth, bird words from sweet lips sooth forth. Exhausted from wing-sweeping, sky by sky, the warbler sips in his liquid sounds.

Clutches of buds brood on the branches as he mothers her into air white with bride signs. Principled by the wild, the bird lights away the fear blinkered into our eyes--even my scarred veins are carried like string to build a nest--*gifts god us and then our god is gone.*

XXVII.
THE FROG CHORUS

Mom is arrayed on the sofa. She's always arrayed on the sofa, except for when she's upright playing solitaire, or eating her half of a banana for breakfast, ice cream sundae for lunch, Stouffer's for dinner. Arrayed on the sofa, Mother takes a drag off her cigarette--the smoke makes a charcoal-grey halo around her face. She looks insect-frail, a Praying Mantis laid out in a sarcophagus, limbs thin as fiddle-bows. The lamp on the table beside her is an examination light, coldly illuminating her heart, which is a dark speck floating in a once fertile egg.

How could I have known that such an insect would hatch from a speck floating in a once fertile egg? Or worse, that eggs die inside the body that hosts them because the body is bound by the failings of flesh--flushed, falling, gorgeous, doomed. Isn't Mom's body, my body, all bodies built with the same beauty in mind?

All in hers is in ruin. Mine isn't much better. My limbs are also fiddle-bow thin. Still in the seizure years, I'm down to ninety-three pounds, am so ill I fear that I won't live to see age fifty. I pray I don't have a seizure now as I take Mom's hands into mine--they're cool as my garden in evening where I drink in dark bins of air, oddly intimate with the green bodies of plants. I planned that beauty, but ours, mine, humankind's--is wrought from wonder and pain.

My mother has been arrayed on the sofa for months, years, centuries, has been waiting for me, her youngest daughter, to come, pay homage, lend her if not love, then a bit of pity. Heavy curtains, like those in a puppet theatre, are drawn closed before sliding glass doors.

Somewhere outside it's summer: large puppets descend long blue hills and evening is introducing its mystery play with marionettes and players who box shadows dense with shadowy souls.

My soul, adorned in such dressy shadows, refuses to mix with Mom's, its smoky wreath. Our own strings twitch as we speak in voices low as a priest's in the coffin of the confessional. I want her to say, "We are of the earth and the earth is of us." I want her to say, "Whatever takes the breath away, the wind will keep," but Mom's words have frogs in them, weeping frogs, and in her few, distant words, the frog chorus resounds.

The frog chorus resounds, is magnified by the cries of frogs out in the yard where they're scattered, like plums fallen from the chilly trees. Suddenly, I feel amphibious--my own skin is soft, permeable as the frogs' cool, nubile flesh.

Perhaps I, who live above and below, have come to escort Mother to her permanent underworld. Am I meant ensoul her, strand by strand, in a web that's a bright hope easily undone, a fabric transient as tears? Or am I here to receive her few, distant words, words created by the machinations of not just a ruined body, but a brain so bleak, it's stained with soot.

"Canaries," I say, and she looks at me stupefied. Everything stupefies Mom--the tying of shoes, the fork and the spoon, even the solitaire she plays incessantly--the slap of the cards on the coffee table, the only music she can make on an earth that no longer wants her, perhaps never did.

"I love canaries," I continue, yet what I want to say is, "Mom, please die faster than me." What I want to say is, "May we never meet again." Instead I blurt, "I love canaries because they sing in the bleakest of mines."

She looks at me dumbfounded. I don't blame her. I reach to cup her face, its tarnished relic, but she flinches, as if struck by a blow.

Mom's dying, a death begun in earnest when Dad went to the other side. No one knows she's dying but me, yet it's true--already her dishrag soul's tugging its way out of her body, knot by knot, amid the uproarious frog chorus.

Even Mom doesn't know she's dying, When she speaks, she speaks in frog. I expect her to say, "I'm about to croak," but she doesn't. Rather, I feel her breath--it's amphibious: dank with sour cells that age with each froggy breath. She doesn't even comprehend her words--frog language is weighty, webbed with that fabric transient as tears. When I remind her I'm a poet, she looks at me as if I've cursed.

"Too bad," she croaks, and I expect a frog or two to pop out of her mouth, blue frogs with yellow polka dots. When no frogs with yellow polka dots pop out, I take out my poet's pen, draw a face on the side of my right index finger and thumb, make a hand puppet.

I open, close the puppet mouth. "O fickle foe," I say, "let's make pickle dough."

When I get no response from Mom, I go on, "Bim-bam-boodle, I'm in love with a noodle." Still no response, so I add, "Poodle-pie is divine because it's baked in sunshine."

"In what?" asks Mom.

"Sunshine," I reply, "merry sunshine." I pause, "I told you I was a poet. This is what you and Dad put me through college for."

Mom cracks a smile.

"I even graduated Magna Cum Laude," I add.

"At least," she croaks, "our money went somewhere."

I give her a thumb's up. She gives me one back. "Oh, I guess, you want to thumb wrestle?"

Her thumb goes down. Mom's too weak to thumb wrestle. For that matter, I'm too weak to thumb wrestle, so I do what I never thought I would do--I who have made a pilgrimage of a thousand miles to see a mom whom I'll soon remember struck me upside the head with a bat--over the body of this woman whom no one loves, not even the frog chorus, I awkwardly make the sign of the cross.

I bless her, am stricken as she lifts her cocktail glass, stares at its gold fire as though it's the spirit of her one and only God, a God who refuses her the selfsame blessing.

Mom's melting, like paraffin. If God refuses to bless her, then I have because in doing so, I've proffered that blessing upon myself. By blessing myself, I'm bloodletting her. This bloodletting sucks her soul into the heaviest of clouds.

"Clouds are cows," I say, yet what I want to say is, "Mom, even Christ wouldn't have died for your sins." I want to say, "Mom, Christ wouldn't have died for you or Dad's sins." I want to say, "Did the two of you sacrifice me for your sins?" but don't because that would make me sound crazy--Donald thinks I'm crazy enough, so I keep my thoughts to myself.

Out pops my own frog or two, "Cows jump over the moon," I let out, as if telling a nursery rhyme to a young child while my own child is back home, somewhere in summer, playing with large blue puppets, dancing in between their shadow-boxings.

"I'll box your ears," Mom used to say before whacking me upside the head. Back then, her hair was the color of rage--black hair that matched the black showpiece her ruined brain was, is intent on becoming.

"Peace be with you," are my next words, but there aren't any weeping frogs in them, only the clarity of bells and we all know for whom the bell tolls.

Mom looks stunned, is the bird which flies into the window with a dull thud, or has the window flown into her? A tear--bright, transient--drools from her eye. She quickly wipes it away, as if it were a froggy tear, even though as far as I know, frogs don't weep. They just croak until they croak, as does Mom. Given how sick I am, I may croak, too.

Wishing I were wearing a froggy dress, or a makeshift wetsuit with yellow polka dots, I make a sign of the cross over both of us while she heaves last breaths--heavy, damning breaths that damn her.

That I'll grieve over Mom too long and become grief's numb drum, as I was for her violence, is something I will do, in spite of everything. By doing so, I'm grieving for the mother I never had, the one whose glimmer, like a firefly, loitered in one part of her body until she extinguished it, as she now does now with the butt of her cigarette.

I'll go through the grief I endured when Dad died because I grieved the death of his glimmer, too. I'll let my sorrow become succor, which makes me what I am--a manifestation of the divine.

"Amen," I croak, while half-expecting Mom to literally croak.

Instead of croaking, I hear her cells zoom out of her like tiny, black comets in a room that's still as the eye of a tornado. As I'm back in tornado country, I know there's one skirmishing on the distant horizon. I love tornado country, how the sky turns into green gruel just before one hits, recall the drills we practiced in school--we hid under our desks, or were herded into an underground corridor where we were made to pray.

Right now, I'm made to pray because prayer blesses me. I do so silently as I leave Mom, there on the sofa, where she's a lady-in-waiting who's waiting for death to wait on her hand and foot. As I leave, I know I'll never see her again and by doing so, it's akin to leaving tornado country for good.

XXVIII.
CLICK, CLICK

Because Donald's exhausted from my illness, I urge him to go on vacation in the Galapagos Islands. As soon as Donald leaves the country and is out of reach of all communication, Mom becomes sicker than me, much sicker. She's sick enough to almost croak in the driveway where Gene, who's driven down from Wisconsin to help her, picks her up, performs a sad pas de deux to get her into the car. They go to the hospital where she's admitted, against her will.

I call daily for reports. Gene's vigilant, as is Marie. I'm told Mom is raving, absolutely crazy for a cigarette, a drink. Marie says she's the Wicked Witch of the Midwest. I'm not surprised--are they finally seeing the Mom I knew?

On the following Saturday, nearly a week after Mom's hospitalized, I give her my daily call by picking up the phone, dialing the room number, asking for her. Instead of Gene or Marie, a nurse answers, says that I can't talk to Mother because she's getting her hair washed.

I'm elated--only people who're going to live get their hair washed! Suddenly, the light turns exotic, the stately trees outside my study windows are bronzed with gold. I want to be one of these trees--

they're not just stately, but emanate an elegance from their wounds. These wounds are the shining dark, which is where I long to dwell.

I gaze at the trees the way astronomers do stars. Their broken limbs are akin to my own brokenness. I notice how their brokenness is what truly puts them into alignment, the way my words align themselves in poems. My work is to study, to articulate, carefully, the gorgeous void in the shining dark of every wound, to document the audacious capacity each wound has to heal.

Lost or, perhaps, found in my rumination, I hear the doorbell ring. I wonder who it is: very few of our friends--mine, Donald's--stop by without calling first. I go to the red door, open it, see one of my husband's oldest friends, Mary, standing there holding a bag of croissants. Her face is a still life that's hard to read. Then I see Dan--I'm confused, shocked. Why would Dan fly all the way from his home in North Carolina, to turn up on my front stoop? He looks worried, exhausted.

"Why are you here?" I ask. It's a question that presupposes a logical answer, or an acceptable one.

"It's Mom," he says. I want to reach up to caress his brow, smooth away the worry lines.

"She's fine," I reply, in a breezy voice, "I just called--she's getting her hair washed." I say this with assurance, insistence. Birds are pipping in the nearby trees, each sound pops, like a burst bubble. I feel Ryan draw near, flank me. He's a stick-to-me kid. I'm glad he is, as I'm a stick-to-my-kid Mom. Because of the bird pips, all I want to do is blow bubbles with him, a long cascade of bubbles that'll float up into the flyways.

"Ryan," I start, "do you want to blow some bubbles? Dan, Mary, you can, too."

"Elizabeth," says Dan.

"What?" I reply, not liking how leaden my name sounds. I'm pretty sure it has the force of gravity in it, will pull me under, so I say, "We love blowing bubbles, just to watch them pop."

"She's gone," he continues. I'm wondering who he's talking about. Maybe he's referring to Gene's old cat, Dorothy.

"Who's gone where?" My voice is wobbling. The clouds look salty.

"Mom," he says.

It dawns on me, no, it eclipses me: Mom isn't getting her hair washed because Mom's dead. Dead people don't get their hair washed.

"But the nurse," I offer in sorrow.

"Mom would've wanted a family member to tell you. That's why I'm here, to tell you in person. She died last night."

The air thins. I start to shake, fear a seizure will seize me. I grab Ryan's hand to help steady myself. Dead, deader, deadest. I need Donald, but he can't be reached. Besides, he's remarked that he doesn't expect me to attend either of his parents' funerals, a remark I found disturbing.

"Okay," I say. In that instant, grief returns. Time blurs, air slurs. I move as though wearing cement boots. Over Mary's croissants, we make preparations, pack, then fly into the heart of the country to attend the funeral.

In the church, I have trouble walking, begin to go into a seizure. Dan grips my thin arm, seats me. At seven, Ryan's a pall bearer---he smiles at me while coming up the aisle heaving Mom's casket into church, clearly proud he's doing a good job. In that moment, I remember how a butterfly once mistook his strawberry blonde hair for a flower, alighted upon his head. In that moment, pollen shines the graceless air until it gleams chartreuse, even though September's closing its leafy doors.

Only Dan, Marie, Gene and I congregate at the cemetery where Mom's urn--she has been cremated--will be buried next to Dad's grave. In the nearby field, a scarecrow thins, as if impaled upon its post. The corn has been shorn. The grey stubble looks like broken pieces of PCV pipe while crows, those assiduous suitors, party hearty, clout the gunmetal sky.

"We're it," Dan says, "we're the elders now that Mom and Dad are gone," then adds, "God broke the mold when he made them."

We agree by bowing our heads down, as if in prayer, but none is offered, unless one counted the crows' caws as sacred. No tears are shed, no frogs croak. No words are wasted because their deaths have wasted a part of us, as did their lives.

Dan flies Ryan and me back home because I'm too sick to travel by myself, let alone with a child. I'm in a seizure most of that long flight and melt, like a figure in a Dali painting, in my seat. Dead, deader, deadest is how I feel, too.

Mary meets us at the gate. I turn to say goodbye to Dan.

"You're stellar," I say, "to do this for me, just stellar." I then fold my hands in prayer, bow my head--not like a sinner, but like a woman with a holy name, whisper, "Peace."

"Thank you, Little Bits," Dan replies. He then says, "You know if Mom had been there, she'd have ducked out of church before the end of her own funeral Mass."

"You're right," I say, laughing, "she always ducked out of church early."

"Yes, she did," and with that, he smiles, turns away.

A few days later, Donald calls from Miami. He's on the way home.

"Mom's dead," I say, "it was hard not having you with me at the funeral."

"Sorry" he replies, "but I had a wonderful trip. See you soon."

I hear a click, but no goodbye. This is typical. No matter how many times I implore Donald not to hang up without saying goodbye, he does so anyway. Just a click. *Click, click,* but not the click poets love, the one we hear when a poem is done. *Click,* dead, deader, deadest.

When Donald does come home, he gives me a stiff, formal hug, then proceeds to tell about being in the water with a hammerhead shark. He knew enough to back away slowly and took a photo, *click,* while doing so. It's then, *click,* I realize that Mom was the hammerhead and in the moment when my husband shot the photo, *click,* she died. *Click, click.*

XXIX. ELIZABETH PLAYS I SPY

It's late afternoon and I'm cutting potatoes for the kale soup because my little family loves kale soup. I'm cutting potatoes for the soup, the peels slick, wet autumn leaves, their meat, white as cornstarch. Suddenly, the knife flies out of my hand. It flies out of my hand while that cruel wizardry fires up my arm to storm my body. Quick as breath, I go down onto the floor, am a kite, wind-knocked, sky-shattered. Wind-knocked, I go down while my limbs flail in a full-blown seizure.Flailing, I'm half on, half off the orange rug with night animals on it--black owls, black cats, crows.

Half on, half off, the orange rug with the night animals on it, I'm in a seizure. My Savage Maker scurries into a cellar hole where his teeth chatter in darkness. This chattering Savage Maker is a puppeteer. He jerks my limbs, a marionette, by invisible strings, causing me to flail even more.

Jerked by invisible strings, I flail, stare up into the skylight as though it's a spyglass and think, *It's time to play I Spy*. I want to shout, *I spy black owls!* I want to shout, *I spy black cats and crows in their priestly robes!* but I can't speak when in a seizure, let alone shout. And so, I spy nothingness, the abyss, and the loneliness that saddens molecules, but I do not spy my My Savage Maker, no, I never do when in a seizure.

I do spy my young son sitting down beside me. Seven or eight, Ryan is sitting crosslegged alongside me where I flail on the orange rug with the night animals on it. Seven or eight, he feeds me my meds, like teeny-weeny communion tablets. My young son feeds me my communion, then opens a book to read aloud while the meds kick in.

What he reads aloud are not fairytales. No, they're not tales full of magical enchantment, but almost fairytales and fairly stupid ones at that. Surely my illness is not a fairytale, but a bewitchment.

My son reads, *The hen is screaming.* He reads, *Who will plant the wheat?* Clearly, I'm not screaming because I can't speak let alone scream, nor can I plant the wheat. Ryan keeps reading: *Now the hen is running to Chickin' Lickin', screaming, The sky is falling! Now she's running to Ducky Lucky, then Goosy Lucy, screaming, The sky is falling! We must tell the President!*

Not screaming, I'm spying the skylight--what I see is that the sky isn't falling, no, the sky isn't falling in my fairly stupid fairytale, so there's no need to tell the President. I, however, have fallen into seizure. Not only have I fallen, I've fallen many times before, will many times more, but there's no need to tell the President. I do, however, need to tell my Savage Maker, yet I can't speak, can only hear his mole's teeth chattering in darkness. Do I scare my Savage Maker when I go into seizure? Is that why he scurries into a cellar hole? If so, I understand because I scare myself, too. Why haven't I scared my young son?

Maybe I haven't scared my young son because he's the narrator of this tale. As the narrator, he says, *Yo, just come,* to the frantic hen. Where, *yo*, does he want the frantic hen to come? I want to come with the frantic hen, but, *yo,* how can I when I'm seizing? I want to ask, *Just where, yo, do you want us to come?* but can't.

I want to come with the frantic hen to where, *yo,* Ryan wants her to because that might be the kingdom come. I, a frantic hen, want to go to the kingdom come because, *yo,* the littlest angel might be there to cure me, not preserve me the way hospital rooms do. If, *yo,* the littlest angel cures me, the frantic hen, in the kingdom come, then our fairly stupid tale will have a fairly happy ending.

Before we get to where the littlest angel can cure me, my young son stops reading. He stops reading to lay his hands upon me. When he lays his hands upon me, he's more patient than sorrow. I praise him. I praise him and his hands, the palms plump as small buttocks. I praise his hands' sweat, light as the drizzle glazing the skylight.

The glazing drizzle is a hard sugar. My seizing body is hard, too, but when my young son lays his hands upon me, it starts to melt into the sugars of grief. When I melt, my toes go quiet, like ten small peninsulas. When my toes go quiet, we're bathed in the scent of basements and plums.

Smelling of basements and plums, Ryan's hands multiply, like loaves and fishes. Like loaves and fishes, they're everywhere on my body--my legs, go quiet, then my back and neck. Even my heart goes quiet. My quiet heart is a genie slipped back in its bottle. When my heart is back in its bottle, the bewitchment ends. When the bewitchment ends, so does the fairly stupid tale. The magical enchantment begins.

When the enchantment begins, I get up off the floor, brush crumbs and fish scales off my apron, bow slightly before my young son. I praise him, go back to slicing potatoes for the kale soup. Yes, I praise him and the soup, but I do not praise my Savage Maker. I praise his likeness, here in my kitchen, my kingdom come, am happy that this kingdom, at least for now, has a fairly happy ending.

XXX.
HOW TO MASSACRE THE LITTLE VILLAGE

Be like Mom.

Or be like me, helping my son sort out his stuffed animals. He has many stuffed animals. He has so many stuffed animals, he could fill an ark. There's a hammock full of animals strung from one corner of his room, like a big, blue Spiderman web. They peer out of drawers, from under the bed and on top of it. They cover his white dresser, are watchmen on his towers of books--there's even a cart-load in the closet. These stuffed animals are his little village, but I think he needs more space.

"How about the clown?" I ask. "You've never really liked the clown, right?"

"I guess not," Ryan answers in a still, small voice. He's sitting on his bed with his knees drawn into his chest. He pulls the moon and stars comforter over his stockinged feet, warming them, like two small loaves.

I drop the clown into a black trash bag. Mom used to stuff wrapping paper barely ripped off cheap Christmas gifts into similar trash bags. She did this while sitting in a victory V on the raked, blue shag carpet during Christmases brief as peace.

"What about this guy?" I go on, "does he even have a name?"

"Skunkie," comes Ryan's still, small voice.

"Puey," I respond, as Skunkie is swallowed up in the increasingly pregnant black trash bag.

How to massacre the little village?

Be like Mom

Or be like me, methodically, mechanically going through every animal in my son's room. The ark gets emptied, the little village smaller, but I think we're doing a great job.

"Nice work," I conclude, "you still have Sealy, Gund and Scoopy, plus a few more friends. That should about do it."

"I guess," comes Ryan's even stiller, smaller voice.

"I'm going to donate these to your old preschool now," I announce while swinging the black sack over my back, like the Grinch who stole Christmas, or worse, like Mom hauling out the garbage bag stuffed with wrapping paper.

How to massacre the little village?

Be like Mom.

Or me?

Next morning, I go into Ryan's room, wake him for school. As always, I open the Venetian blinds, such that the light, pale as baby Jesus, can seep in. I sidestep towers of books, newly devoid of their stuffed animal watchmen, place a kiss, wistful as love, on my son's smooth cheek.

He blinks his eyes open, as if from deep meditation.

"Morning, sweetie," I say, "it's time to rise and shine."

My boy's lower lip starts trembling.

"What is it?" I ask, worried.

The lip trembles some more--he starts crying. "My stuffed animals," he sputters, "you massacred them."

"What?" I ask, not sure I heard him right.

"You massacred my stuffed animals," Ryan repeats, crying while clutching those still in his possession. "Where's Skunkie and Al? What happened to Mr. Turtle and Care Bear? Where's my big, blue Spiderman web to hold them all."

"But," I start, "remember we went through them together?"

My boy ducks under his stars and moon cover, "You massacred my stuffed animals," he says once more in the stillest, smallest, voice under heaven.

How to massacre the little village?

Be like Mom.

Or be me, a mom who goes to her distressed child, in the pale as baby Jesus light, gathers him in her arms to hold and comfort until his sorrow turns into succor while all the Mary birds up-flutter in the Mary sky.

XXXI. WALKING WITH WINTER

Years pass after my mother passes, but only six months after the seizures stop, I'm in my study writing. My hands are bridled to the keyboard as I tap, tap the keys, spewing words as though each were a dot in a connect-the-dot picture. Mine aren't connecting--each is a dead star in a dead constellation, or a balloon about to pop floating in the hard winter sky, which is the color of concrete. My brain also feels like concrete, cold concrete, or a sheet of ice, and I'm falling across it the way I fell to the floor during the seizure years. Icy, concrete brain, dead as the dead of winter, which is what it is out there and in here, it isn't much better.

My boy turned eleven today, yet I'm fading away, sliding in my brain of winter in this winter of discontent now turning into a winter of disconnect. Dot, dot, like Rorschach tests while I tap, tap, trying to find the line that'll serve as lifeline, keep me tethered to the world, my suburban home. I pause, look out the window, a window hard as a bulletproof vest, start to write again, words like bullets firing away, as if on a rampage. Suddenly, I pull myself erect in my chair as the word *die* fires into my deadhead, deadbeat brain, *die, die.*

This seems like a good idea, the best idea I've had all day. Time, yes, high time, to down my meds, go into the fetal position, turn into a dust baby. That's what's going on in my head, *dust baby, dust baby.* I'm also wrestling with my Savage Maker in an abyss closed shut with a sewer lid--limb upon limb, we pin each other in sewage.

After my Savage Maker and I pin each other, I get up to down all my meds, like eenie weenie communion tablets, but hesitate long enough to dump them into toilet, flush away. I go to the phone, pick it up, but don't know what to do. I'm confused by all the buttons with numbers and letters scrambled on them, like Scrabble pieces which can't be spelled into a word.

Who should I call? A light goes on in my deadbeat brain. I remember a number, punch it in. *Ring-a-ding-ding,* I'm playing the telephone game, but what exactly is the message I'm supposed to send? Someone on the other end, way far away on the other end, picks it up, says, "Dr. Donald Frost," but who the hell is Dr. Donald Frost? Can he help me fix my deadbeat brain? I don't know, so I whisper, "Dust baby," hang up.

Next thing I know Dr. Donald Frost is standing in my study, asking me if I'm okay in an overly concerned voice. I turn to him, say, "Let's play Doctor."

Dr. Frost looks very worried now, his brow is furrowed, his face is growing paler by the second. "You'll be fine," he says, then off into the bedroom he goes where *he* starts to play the telephone game. Slowly I remember who Dr. Donald Frost is--he's my husband, father of my son, Ryan, who turned eleven today.

If it's my son's birthday and it is, I have to bake the birthday cake. Into the kitchen I go where I put on my little helper apron, open the utensil drawer, pull out the butcher knife. It's shiny and beautifully sharp with a razor edge. I'm puzzling over what to do with the knife when Dr. Donald Frost comes in.

"Hi Donald," I say, like a normal mother and wife, "I'm going to bake Ryan's birthday cake."

"No," he says, as he eases the knife out of my hand, "we're going to the hospital."

I burst into tears, shake my head *no, no,* not on my son's birthday, insist on baking the cake before Ryan comes home from school. Donald guides me out of the kitchen and into the bedroom where he takes out my black, ratty overnight bag. In goes my boy's teddy bear, Gund, a picture of me as a Dust Baby, my flannel nightgown, slippers.

"A field trip!" I exclaim, "we're going on a field trip."

"Yes," Donald replies and off we go with me feeling like a free spirit.

We get in the car, drive in silence until we pull up to Beth Israel Hospital in downtown Boston. I tap my finger to my temple, the one with the birthmark on it, turn to Donald, say, in an expert voice, "This is where my baby was born."

"Yes," he says in that worried tone, but I assume we're here to visit the maternity ward. When I step out of the car, I say, *tra-la-la,* as if I'm Cinderella going to an enchanted ball.

Instead of taking me to the maternity ward, or the ball, Donald escorts me into the ER where we're escorted into a room behind a "Let's Make a Deal" curtain. Is my son blowing out the candles on the birthday cake I didn't get to make? Should I sing the birthday song even though we're in the ER?

I don't sing the birthday song because I want to scream. I want to scream because my dust baby is being blown to smithereens and my Savage Maker is pinning me down in piss and shit.

I yell, *Monkey, I cry monkey!* At this, doctor after doctor comes in. They ask me perfectly absurd questions, which I don't know the answers to.

Who cares what year it is, or who the hell the President is? I know it's Ryan's birthday--isn't this enough? Another doctor comes in, asks me to sign a sheet of paper which will voluntarily put me in the psych ward.

I burst into tears again, shake my head, *no,* tell the doctor that I can't possibly go into the psych ward on my son's birthday, but all too soon, my bed is being wheeled out of the ER.

I look back, see a very sad Dr. Donald Frost turn away, hear my heart break. It's breaking really hard, like the Little Match Girl's last matchstick. My heart is breaking and breaking some more, like that matchstick and I know it'll never stop breaking. I know I'll never be the same again, feel this with all of my broken heart as the doors to the unit open and I'm wheeled across the red line, the one I won't be allowed to cross for too many days on end, the red line that's ten feet behind the locked doors to which *they,* the anonymous *they* of doctors and nurses, my keepers, have thrown away the key.

I'm given anti-psychotics, like the communion I almost downed, sleep until 4:00 a.m., only to leap out of bed, put on my slippers to start pacing down the guarded hallway and back. The pacing is important. I don't know why I have to pace down the guarded hallway and back, but I do so for two hours, until the community room opens at 6:00 a.m., where I drink tea, eat Graham Crackers.

For my entire hospital stay, I pace every morning from 4:00 to 6:00 a.m., only to eat Graham Crackers, drink tea. For my entire hospital stay, I watch my husband cross the red line, as he leaves after a visit, during which I sit in my stuffed monkey body, my lips stitched shut. Sometimes he holds one of my cold hands. Sometimes he plants a kiss on my stuffed monkey forehead, but mostly I feel his sadness, his enormous sadness, over losing the woman of his choosing and receiving a woman who's lost it all, including her mind. I vaguely think that he needs more help than I do, he who, sadly, has stood by me through more sickness than health with more sickness to come. I watch him cross the red line, hunched over like someone in grief, vaguely wonder who he's grieving for.

It's nearing Christmas. I hoard quarters to make calls out, hide them in an old sock so they won't get stolen. When I speak to Ryan, I try to sound chipper, even though I'm hollowed out inside.

Hollowed out, I ask, "Why did Beethoven kill his chicken?"

"I don't know, Mom, why?" he replies.

"Because it kept clucking, *Bach, Bach,"* I say, in a super chipper voice, yet what I want to say is, "I'm sorry I didn't bake your birthday cake." I want to say, "I'm sorry I missed your birthday," or, "I'm terribly sorry you have a crazy Mom." Instead, I say, *bye-bye,* in the stillest, smallest voice under heaven.

Tearily, I wear my flannel nightgown and hospital socks with the lime-green smiley faces on them during my entire hospital stay. Tearily, I stand at night by the suicide-proof window in my room, longing to leap out of it, just to feel the beauty of falling in breathtaking air.

Instead, I gaze into another hospital room in a different ward. There, an old woman massages the back of an even older man under the stern glow of the ceiling light. I wish them the respite deep within the silent hearts of snowflakes then falling like hordes of white butterflies into the river below, but more than that, I want to be back in the maternity ward where I had birthed my son eleven winters before.

After a small eternity, the day before my release comes. On that day, my body drifts, like a barge, through locks in a dam into the community room where the TV is always on--the screen livid with the news blaring, graphic as porn--it blasts into the outer space of my inner space. There are no windows in the community room. My barge of a body sinks into the sofa, the pillows, cold, cold waves, when suddenly, I feel under siege because the dust*--or is it my Dust Baby?*--is having a seizure. It snorts out of the blaring, flaring nostrils of the dragon who stalked me during the seizure years, yet how does one drug the dust, or worse, the Dust Baby? Dimly, that drugged dust settles on the barge of my body which is heavily drugged. Before me is the collage of the giant snowman we made in Arts and Crafts--I understand, with great clarity, how every snowman is abominable, as is every snow-woman.

In enters another inmate, Victoria, tiny, regal as a peacock with black eyeliner crusted around cobalt eyes. Her hair, dark as a nighttime meadow, is swept up. Her age is her rage. She sits next to me on the sofa. We talk, quietly, while our hearts float up, like magnets to the same pane of glass.

"I have a poem," she says with a deliberately French accent.

"Oh," I reply, "I'd love to see it."

She hands me a piece of paper folded into a dainty origami bird. Victoria is like that bird--made of paper folded too tight, thin paper that threatens to tear if touched, so I don't touch her, not even her slim fingers which remind me of Chinese finger-pulls.

"Thank you," I say, "thank you very much," as I delicately unfold the bird, wing by wing.

I spread the tissue-thin sheet of paper on my lap, smooth it, iron it lightly with the warmth of my fingertips. Upon it are three words, just three words, crafted in script so careful the letters singe the page. I read the words aloud, *Walking with Winter.*"

Victoria winces, then smiles. "That's just the title," she offers, "I can't go any further."

I pause, feel my eyes deepen with sadness. "No," I reply, "that's the whole poem."

"Really?" she asks.

"Really," I answer, let go with a sigh.

Victoria pats my hand. "Thank you," she says as though she's Grandma. O how I long to be with Grandma, here on my last day in the unit. I need her to tell me how I'm still her guardian angel. She'd tell me this before walking with me, arm-in-arm. We'd walk everywhere together--back to the World's Fair where we stood in the Wall of People and I met Carby Carburetor. We'd even walk back to her funeral where I sang her favorite song, "O Happy Day," even though my happy days are gone, seemingly for good. Still, it's with her that I wish to cross the red line into a world so bright I'll nearly keel over.

Quietly, Victoria retrieves her poem, folds it back into an origami bird that can't fly. Of course it can't fly, who could when walking with winter? Victoria walks with winter right out of the community room, her tiny, regal head raised a bit higher. In emptiness, I stare at the snowman on the wall, am the abominable snow-woman who walks with winter, too, will continue to walk with winter for many years to come.

In some ways, I never leave the lock-up. There remains the remains of me toeing the red line, its brilliant line of poetry. Forevermore, I watch the small sail of my husband's shirt disappear through the locked doors, am left bereft in my flannel nightgown. In that nightgown, I fight off predatory shadows with a ward chair, tear into confetti the book I can't write, wail in a pitch that could have cracked Grandma's good china. Because of this, I'll do Art Therapy in the selfsame unit I never leave.

I never see Victoria again. Early the next day, I rise, shakily, out of dreams, only to become Plath's Lady Lazarus. I pad down, in my flannel nightgown, to the nurses' station where I pester them all day by asking when Donald's due to arrive. "Go away," they say, over and over, swatting at me, like a pesky fly.

What the keepers took away from me upon admission--sharps, cords, anything with which I could do myself harm--is returned. Other inmates mill about me like sleepwalkers, practiced somnambulists, as if we're having a farewell party on a gravesite. "Who's dead?" I'm dying to ask, deeply afraid it might be me, but I swallow my words because they might sentence me to more time behind the red line.

When my husband does arrive, I say, "Wait, please," before walking down the hall to where a man who isn't allowed to leave his room, stands in the doorway round the clock, like a scarecrow, or harrowed Christ. The air is starched yellow. The pain between us is palpable because *love is to pain what pain is to love.* He's a tailor, loves to draw but the anonymous *they,* the anonymous *they,* our keepers, refuse to give him paper or pen. I look at him. Shadows inside shadows hide in his eyes. I give him the legal pad and pen Donald brought to me so I could write, but my poem remains a Wagnerian song without words. This scarecrow man, this New Age aging Christ, starts to cry. I take his hand in mine, bring it to my lips, kiss it, say, "Peace be with you."

Immediately, a male keeper is upon me. He yells at me, tells me this scarecrow man, this Christ, is violent. I sigh, step away, walk back down the corridor where my sad husband patiently waits. Together we cross the red line, its brilliant line of poetry, but not for good.

Outside, the light is so bright, my eyelids threaten to peel. The sky is cobalt, like Victoria's eyes, the clouds lit by the breath of my once-upon-a-time fiery dragon. I think, or want to think, I hear heralding trumpets.

As soon as I get home, I rush down to the school to greet my eleven year old boy. There I swing him so high, I think he might forgive me. We walk home through crunchy snow, talking non-stop.

When we open the red door to our home, Ryan says, "Close your eyes." I do. He guides me into the living room, spins me around to make me dizzy. "Now open," he says. I do. Before me is the Christmas tree he and his father put up without me, resplendent the way Christmas trees are with shining lights, ornaments, garlands. Ryan points to the coffee table where my favorite ornament lies in red tissue. It's an angel holding a watering can. When he says softly, "I saved this for you," my huge, broken heart starts breaking again.

That night, instead of listening to Christmas music, we play the CD Ryan loves so well, the one with Bobby McFarrin and Yo Yo Ma on it. We put on what we call "The Bumble Bee Music," soar all over the house, buzzing, flying away. We play that track over and over, do our Bumble Bee dance as we've done for years until, at last, we flop flat on the floor, kick our hands and feet in the air, cry out, "Alleluia!" as we break down laughing, laughing all the way, while winter briefly vanishes.

XXXII.
ELIZABETH STAYS OUT OF THE LOCK-UP ONE WHOLE YEAR

On the evening of my first anniversary of staying out of the lock-up one whole year, I open the red door to the house. It gives way with a dispassionate heave. The winter moths, clustered on the outdoor lamp, scatter like tiny dunces, or the snow just now falling. While the winter moths scatter like dunces, or falling snow, I step into the foyer whose floor consists of smooth-as-tortoiseshell slate. I can't help but long for my once architectural mind to be just as smooth as the slate. I long for it to have not been broken into stony pieces, a chaos of pieces, like the letters of an illiterate alphabet no one can understand, not myself, or my dead, not even the small god of my understanding.

My architectural mind hasn't only been broken, it's also been muffled into an echo. Perhaps, my mind has been muffled because it can't tolerate the crucible of memory it now retrieves in fits of madness, wild as this snow, just now falling.

No one can understand this broken mind of mine, not myself, nor my dead, or my god because, in retrieving bits of memory in madness, I've been retrieving pieces of a childhood no one would want to remember. Who would want to remember such a childhood, especially when its memories are retrieved in fits of madness that aren't just terrifying, but excruciating? Who, just who? No one, absolutely no one, so I tell no one about these memories, especially not my husband or son.

Still, as I stand in the foyer on tortoiseshell slate, I'm not remembering the crucible of a childhood retrieved in madness, but the fact that I've stayed out of the lock-up one whole year, despite these mad fits and the broken, stony pieces of my mind. I'm remembering I've stayed out of the lock-up one whole year and that I've asked Donald to buy me a gift to celebrate this feat.

I breathe in air so thin, it's flat, like champagne without bubbles--it's the only air available, the way the shadowy light in the foyer is the only available light. I borrow this thin, flat air, shadowy light, as if I could give it back, the way the moon, fat as a peony, does.

In the kitchen, a drawer opens and closes. I remember, for no reason, that I love the spoon better than the knife because spoons make music and knives do not. I relish this thought, almost dash into the kitchen to grab a spoon to make a little music with, or to spoon some mudlicious sweetness into me. Perhaps, if I spooned some mudlicious sweetness into me, then my life would be yummy and edible again, as it once was with Grandma.

I don't grab a spoon to spoon some sweetness into me because it's winter, not spring, and there's only chaotic snow falling on an unmuddy, unlicious earth. Instead, I call out a quiet hello to the shadowy figure that is my husband as he moves from the granite kitchen counter to the granite kitchen table.

They say that diamonds win the hardness factor among gems--does granite win the hardness factor among stones? It is terribly unforgiving. Is Donald just as unforgiving? If he is unforgiving, what do I need his forgiveness for? My madness, or the crucible of a childhood no one would want to remember? If he's unforgiving, am I? Will both of us win the hardness factor?

"Hello, Donald," I say, because "hello" is a word that can't be ridiculed, yet no "hello" comes back, only a muffled echo.

"I'm home," I call out, as I take off my coat, boots, slip on my boiled wool slippers. I move silently in my slippers--silent is good, can't be ridiculed, even young children understand this. I would do anything to please Donald--if that means bleeding silence for him, I'll bleed it, miles and piles of silence because even young children understand how important it is not just to be pleasing but *silent.* Perhaps, if I had been a pleasing, silent child, I'd have no memories to retrieve in chaotic madness. Because no memories equals no madness, there'd be no need for my being put back in the lock-up ever again.

I walk up the stairs to go to my husband. I walk upstairs to go to my husband because it is the work of wives to do so. I go to him to give him a kiss, light as a pea, because it is the work of wives. Donald is tall, so I need to look up to him--he wants this, all men do.

When I look up, I whisper, *Sorry.* I say *sorry* to Donald in a sorry, little voice because I'm afraid he won't forgive me. I'm afraid he won't forgive me for my childhood memories, or my madness, and so, I apologize to him. A lot. *Sorry,* I say again, then add, "did you remember?"

Donald shrugs his shoulders as if they itch. "No," he says, "I forgot."

As he shrugs, I feel like a hurt little cuckoo bird. Not only do I feel like a hurt cuckoo bird, but this cuckoo bird actually is cuckoo.

Even if I'm a hurt little cuckoo bird who's cuckoo, how could Donald forget to buy me a gift? How could he not understand how much a hurt cuckoo-cuckoo bird needs a gift for staying out of the lock-up one whole year? O how I need him to hold his cuckoo bird dearly, closely. O how I need him to say, "I love you, my cuckoo bird, dearly, deeply." I need him to say, "I'm proud of you for staying out of the lock-up."

But there's no gift, no embrace, not even any dearness from Donald, even though I had shyly, no, apologetically, asked for one. Didn't I work hard in order to stay out of the lock-up? Didn't I work hard by walking with winter, day in, day out, for one whole year? And won't I have to walk with winter, day in, day out, for many more winters to come before learning how to stay out of the lock-up for good? Yes, yes, yes.

Because there's no gift, no embrace, nor dearness from Donald, this little cuckoo bird breaks down. I begin to cry. Crying, I run out of the kitchen and into our bedroom. Once in our bedroom, I ball up, balling, on our bed. I ball up, balling, on the marital bed, that flightless island I can't sail around to reach the husband I desperately need, not a gift from, but love. Little bits of love for the Little Bits that's me.

I cry for that little bit of love, pitifully, pathetically, not just like a hurt little cuckoo bird, but one whose heart and mind are broken. I cry and cry, until my face is soggy. I cry until my pillow is soggy--the bed is soggy, as are the walls, the clouds, the fat peony moon. Heaven is soggy, too, as are the angels, fallen or otherwise. Even my god, my Savage Maker, is soggy. My Savage Maker is so soggy he's as pitiful and pathetic as me.

If my Savage Maker is as pitiful as me, then maybe, he'll forgive me, not just for a childhood no one would want to remember and my fits of madness, but also for needing the gift my husband forgot to get. If my soggy Savage Maker forgives me, can I forgive him? What do I need to forgive him for? For letting me become a cuckoo-cuckoo bird in the first place?

Before I can figure this out, the shadowy figure of my husband appears in the doorway. By now, my soggy cuckoo brain is foggy. In my soggy, foggy brain, I don't see Donald in the doorway, but the shadowy figure of my father. Suddenly, I'm back in the kindercoffin, donned in my skeleton costume.

Dad is snapping his belt, saying, "Little Bits, I'm coming to get you." He snaps this his belt again, adds, "Little Bits, this is what you'll get if you don't comply."

Because I think Dad is snapping his belt, ready to come get me, I'm terrified, so much so, I stuff my soggy pillow into my mouth to stop myself from screaming.

Terrified, I don't hear the shadowy figure of my husband call my name, *Elizabeth, Elizabeth.* All I hear is Dad snapping his belt, saying, "Little Bits, look out." When Donald calls my name again, *Elizabeth, Elizabeth,* my soggy, broken cuckoo brain starts to come back.

As I come back, I hear Donald say, *Elizabeth, Elizabeth,* and remember, distantly, that this is my name. I'm proud of remembering my name, the way a precocious child is when she recites her numbers properly. Wasn't I one such precocious child?

"Elizabeth," Donald goes on, "I didn't forget."

"Forget what?" I return in a wisp of a whisper, as I've forgotten what he's forgotten because Donald always remembers to forget everything, the way I forgot everything, including my childhood memories. Does he forget how to love me? Do I, him?

"The gift," he answers, then pauses, before adding, like a weary parent, "I was only joking."

I sigh. His jokes never make me laugh. This one certainly doesn't. Donald thinks all his jokes are funny, even though he never gets a laugh out of me, or Ryan. Is letting your wife cry until her broken cuckoo brain is so soggy it's foggy actually funny?

"Okay," I say, as I crawl off the bed to go to him. I go to Donald because this is the work of wives, especially wives who've stayed out of the lock-up one year.

I take the gift, whisper, "Thank you," in my sorry voice. I open the gift. There it is--a necklace upon which hangs an onyx pendant studded with faux diamonds.

"It's precious," I say, "too precious. I might break it."

Donald says, *it's not too precious because it's faux.* He says, *you can't break faux,* but all I hear is Mom yelling, "Little Bits, just because you're precocious doesn't mean you're precious." I hear Mom yell, "Little Bits, I'll break up that precocious brain of yours, then we'll see just how damn precious you are," while out comes the bat, the ping pong paddle, pots and pans.

I'm so terrified that when Donald tries to put the necklace on me, I flinch, as if struck by a blow. He just says, "Elizabeth, faux is in."

For a moment, I think he's said "foe," not "faux." For a moment, I think he's my foe. Worse, I think he's my faux foe and if so, does that mean his love is faux? How can I unfoe my faux husband, his faux-foe love?

As my husband helps me with the necklace, I wonder what the hardness factor of faux diamonds is? Surely Donald knows this. He's a scientist. Doesn't every scientist know the hardness factor? Isn't he a brilliant one the way diamonds are, even faux ones?

I don't ask my husband about the hardness factor. Instead, I kiss him. I kiss him because it's the work of wives to do so. It's wife-work to be grateful for what we get, even if it's faux love.

In the end, and there is an end, when his hardness factor wins, isn't it because I've fully softened my Kirschnerized self until I'm too soft to break anymore? Aren't I soft enough to be precious? Still, *Pray tell, love, why aren't I precious to you? Can't you see, love, that you're precious to me? What hardened you? When did you, start to walk with winter, day in, day out, just like me? If you're still walking with winter, I beg you, Stop.*

Five:

KITTERY POINT

2010-2013…

"Butterfly Migration"

XXXIII.
ELIZABETH AMONG THE RELIABLE SPLENDORS

Scott and I, along with his helper, Seth, are rehabilitating my little house. We've been doing so all summer. We're rehabilitating my house with blue eggshells and glue, with bell ropes and nails, with sheet rock and the undersides of song. We're putting in doors, letting out mice, building windows out of dust and crystals, making shingles out of prayer books, mirrors. We're building a chapel, schoolhouse, dollhouse, an utter enchantment that's on schedule and under budget.

I'm strong now. I'm strong forevermore. It's a strength built from the inside out because I let time heal me. I let time heal me by letting the miraculous come close, by breathing in its green balm, exhaling the exhaust my dead exhume. My healing is merciful and comes deeply, slow as salt, fast as fizz. I court my healing by blessing it with ashes and grass. I bow to it--to the north, the south, east, west, making it my essential universe.

Because I go after it, through, under and over my healing, I braid it into the plaits of my being. By doing so, I learn that a mad mind can heal, but a mad soul--Mom, Dad's--can't. My mind is a lighthouse, greenhouse, moonhouse. It's a dream structure built upon a foundation of boulders caulked by starlight and mission figs. I'm not only built to last beyond my own last lasting, but out of a fabric transient as tears, a hope that's not easily undone.

I'm so strong, I can spit nails. Instead, I nail them while my strawberry-blonde hair brushes the elephant ears of my shoulder blades. I'm wearing a muscle shirt, skinny jeans, cowboy boots. When I turn to look at Scott, I smile, showing him my two, front chipped teeth. It's a bright, funny smile. It somehow goes with my smart-girl eyeglasses, my suave curves and curls.

We're working on putting a new roof on my loft, beyond which is a new bathroom, big as a ballroom, right above a dining room that stands where the old lean-to once stood, depressing as the grand depression I used to be in. While I pound away, I realize that the reliable splendors are here, before my eyes--they're in the water's obstinate refusal to be a still life, the garden's gay display of clownish blossoms, in deer tracks fresh as ginger. The reliable splendors are in every little bit of light, its hard shine, that's just as strong as the Little Bits I am and always will be. This makes me a reliable splendor, too.

Scott's busy firing off numbers, as he does all day, every day. "I need three two by sixes," he calls out to Seth. The table saw begins to *whir-whir*. We're determined to get the roof on before the afternoon shuts us down, but when I look up, I see more than the hard shine of light rippling the air--warring storm clouds are blowing in, quickly.

"Uh, Scott," I begin.

"What, woman? We have work to do."

"But the sky," I say, "I'm from Tornado Country and that's where I learned to read the sky."

Scott's hammer pauses, mid-air. "Good God," he utters, "we have to cover your house up, now. Seth, grab every tarp you can."

We hustle up and down ladders, laying tarp, nailing it down while those warring clouds bluster in, turn the sky the color of warty bruises. Suddenly, my Maine is in Kansas and even though Rockford isn't, it's where I return, once my house is battened up, and the storm hits.

Inside, we huddle over coffee while the wind exerts its terrible will. Heavy rains lash the house. When the power blows out, I start to sing. I sing for Scott and Seth the way I had for Sister Grace in

Chorus with my high school sweetheart, Jack. I sing softly, then lift my voice until I'm no longer singing for my storm mates, but with Jack.

I sing about love being nothing but rock, salt and nails, about Luxury Liners weighing twenty tons of steel and a quarter moon in a ten cent town, a town that howls in me, like my own lost hometown, while the storm that tans the hide of my house, fails to rip the tarps off the roof. I sing until the sky goes silent and the storm's calm aftermath stills us.

When the lights blinker back on, we stumble outside, dazed by the light already charging stallion-like up the sky. We feel that stallion rise inside us. Relieved, we hug each other, call it a day. Scott and Seth get in their trucks, head home. I'm already home, in my Kansas in Maine, and *o my beloved, heaven is here.*

XXXIV.
RYAN POPS THE LID OFF THE TIME CAPSULE

"I what?" he exclaims as he pulls off his bright orange cleats at the end of a collegiate Ultimate Frisbee tournament. Both Donald and I like his bright orange cleats because they match his bright orange hair. We may now be divorced, but we still like Ryan's bright orange cleats. We even like each other again.

"You opened my time capsule," I answer, casually, "I buried it by the bandstand in Sinnissippi Park. I was ten at the time and promised myself I'd dig it up in the year 2000."

Ryan looks at me like I'm the stuff of sci-fi. I don't tell him that when I buried the time capsule, I was done with the very century I'd been born in because it no longer mattered if Mom and Dad were horny toads, or mechanical insects with lug bolts for a spine and antennae corkscrewing out of their heads--they belonged to the century I was burying. In that instant, they could no longer harm me because I knew a person could get broken up so badly they couldn't get broken anymore. I was that person. Isn't that why everybody called me Little Bits? *Little Bits,* Mother and Father would call out, *we're coming to get you.*

As I walked home from the bandstand, at age ten, every bit of me took on a hard shine that nothing and nobody could dim. I knew then, that not just me, but everybody was a composite of thousands of other bits of composites. My little bits ranged from raw metals to iodine, from tusk to shoreline, from shelf fungi to the blue scent of rain in my grandmother's hair.

"Well," Ryan asks, "did you dig up the time capsule on the right date?"

"No," I answer, "we did."

"What do you mean?"

"You helped."

He gives me his *really mom?* look.

"You did," I insist, "after we buried my Mom in Rockford, we dug up the time capsule. It was the year 2000, the year I promised I'd dig it up."

"How old was I?"

"Seven or eight," I answer, but I'm back burying the time capsule in dirt soft as the chamois lining the pockets of my father's favorite cardigan, the one whose unraveling unraveled me.

"Don't you remember digging up the time capsule with me?" I ask.

"No, not at all," he replies, "tell me about it."

"Well," I begin, "we were still in our funeral clothes and walked from the old Rockford house through Sinnissippi Woods to the bandstand. It was Indian Summer, on the hot side--the leaves were starting to fall off the stripling pines."

"There was a bandshell?" Ryan asks, somewhat interested, somewhat bored.

"It was a popular spot for the Lawrence Welk crowd," I reply, knowing that Ryan has never heard of Lawrence Welk. I just go on, "We went to the corner where the plaque was and started to dig."

"You're joshing me." he says, then yawns.

"No, I'm not. The time capsule was where I remembered it. You were thrilled."

"I doubt it, Mom."

"Well, you wouldn't let me open it. You popped the lid off. A roar came out, like the North, South, East and West winds were trapped in there, or maybe it was the wind of the soul. It came howling out--our hair stood on end while we were lifted off our feet. We were suspended right there in time and space. Our bodies were superfluous as paper bags, or luminaries. We shape-shifted into pure energy, like sugar water, or just sugar the instant it turns into air. I saw your spirit and you saw mine. Yours wobbled a bit, then appeared like a new moon so pearly bright I blinked. You told me mine was warm and looked like a funny pear. We both laughed. The spell was broken. We hit the ground as if wearing moon boots. There we were laughing in our funeral clothes with you holding the time capsule stuffed with flaky dead moss, a mood ring and magic beans."

"Mom, you're the one who's full of magic beans," Ryan says, sweetly.

"You are too, honey. That's why I love you. Everybody's full of magic beans, don't you think?"

"Sure, Mom."

"I'll see you," I reply, before turning to leave the field to drive home. Donald is smiling, waves, then heads toward his car. Alas, there's no *click*.

"Okay, see you," says Ryan, as he gets up for some post-game stretches.

I get into my car, look skyward where a new moon wobbles. It appears so pearly bright, I blink, blink again. It's still pearly white. So is the wind in my soul, Ryan's, and everybody's else's, including Donald's.

XXXV.
ELIZABETH DOES ART THERAPY

I enter the house, flick on a light, throw down my purse, make a beeline to the bathroom, clutching my gut, "Pee," I cry to Larka, "I have to pee!" Once in the bathroom, I yank down my pants, flop onto the toilet seat while hot pee gushes out in a stream. I start to laugh--not only am I peeing on the bee, but I can't count how many times I've rushed through the door, dashed to the bath, yelling, "Pee, I have to pee" while Larka scampers after me, claws slipping and clattering on the wood floors. Time and time again--after the beach, after yoga, after buying groceries, gardening, seeing Ryan. When do I ever *not* have to pee on the bee? I see the mad dash, again, again, like a repeat blooper, laugh until the dog, who's standing halfway through the door, looks scared.

"You're a lesbian," I declare, as her dark eyes fill with watery desire. The kitty sidles up to the dog, rubs her flank. "You're a lesbian, too," I tell her. I swear I hear a silent hiss, before going on, "we're a happy Lesbian family."

Minutes later, we're in bed--me in my skimpy negligee, Larka and the kitty in their birthday suits. "Who's humping whom?" I call out. I can't resist thinking about putting a picture of the three of us having a menage a trois on a dating website. "Single Divorced Female with Single Lesbian dog and Single Lesbian cat seeking Adult Alpha Male."

In the morning, I get dressed, sip tea, look at the dog, the cat, glance down at what I have on, ask, "What's black and white and read all over?" Quizzical faces, upturned ears. "We are," I answer. Larka looks nervous. "Just look," I say. Larka and Twody do look.

"I'm wearing black--you, Larka, are black and you, Twody are black-and-white. Don't you get it?" Deadpan faces. "We're ready for a photo op." More deadpan faces. "Okay, okay, no photo op, just food." Up go the tails.

Over breakfast, I list my life skills, "Staying out of the nuthouse, mooning the universe, screwing, reading, writing, but not arithmetic, walking *without* winter, cooking, staying out of the nuthouse, digging holes, digging even bigger holes, being a mom," I pause, decide to highlight "being a mom," with yellow marker. I continue working on my list, "laughing hard, laughing loudly, cooking, mooning the universe, reading, walking without winter, writing, doing art therapy."

I want, like a proud student, to post this list on the dating website, alongside the cute bedroom pic of me with the dog and the cat, but think better of it. Rather, I go do art therapy.

Soon, I enter a psych ward, one of the ones I'm so good at staying out of, cross the red line. The walls are yellow, like old cellophane, the floor tiles, dull as nail heads. The air smells of old tears, tears that have scabbed over. I'm here to do art therapy in the community room. Here, the staticky TV is on. Inmates are scattered on the sofa and chairs like crash dummies. Pinned to the community board is a quote from Goethe, the one I had copied, years before, when also in the lock-up, to paste into a journal full of inspiring pictures and sayings I made for Ryan in Arts and Craft.

I read it aloud, "Whatever you do, or dream you can, BEGIN IT NOW, boldness has genius, power and magic in it: BEGIN IT NOW." I look around the room in this holding tank for the damned, don't see a whole lot of boldness or genius before me. Instead, I'm thinking that if fish could be depressed, then I'm in a dime store bowl full of depressed fish. Faces bob, go under, bob again.

"Time to sit in a circle and hold hands," I say to these unhappy campers while wishing I had a plastic sit-upon for each one. I look at them, poor, heavy as gravestones, but here, in the lock-up, you do what you are told. Not doing so can isolate you in your room, or worse, it can mean having an armed guard outside your door, so down go the rumps--big ones, scrawny ones, old ones, young ones.

The ward is a true democracy. We're equals in that the Screamer is the same as the Pacer as is the Cutter, but the keepers are dictators. No sharps or cords, room checks every ten minutes. Even at night, our doors are always left open.

"Hold hands." I say, as though we're in Romper Room. These do-bees lace their fingers together like gnarly daisy chains.

"Do you remember the song I taught you?" I receive slow, dopey nods. "Okay, let's sing it."

I start up, "Boom, boom." A few crackly voices join in--these do-bees really do remember.

"Boom, boom," we chime, "ain't it great to be crazy?" We pause, as if to place an exclamation point in a word bubble in the air between us.

We begin again, "Boom, boom, ain't it great to be crazy? Boom, boom, ain't it great to be nuts like us?"

I hold up my hand, like a baton, for one emphatic moment, then resume, "Be silly and foolish all day long, boom, boom, ain't it great to be crazy?"

We sound pretty good, even though we're starkly off-key. "Again," I say. The faces of these depressed fish start to lighten, even brighten. We sing the same verse over and over. "Boom, boom, ain't it great to be crazy?" Smiles appear on the blank chasms of the faces around me. "Boom, boom, ain't it great to be nuts like us?"

The community room is aloft with a noisy luminosity. "Be silly and foolish all day long," a spittle of laughter comes out. "Boom, boom, ain't it great to be crazy?" A few tooted guffaws. By the end of the next round, we're cracking up.

Suddenly, it's incredibly funny to be crazy. It's stupidly funny to be crazy and nuts like us. It's even loonier to sing about how great it is to be silly, crazy and nuts like us. Laughing about being crazy has genius and power and magic in it. Certainly, *boom,* it is bold, *boom, boom.*

XXXVI.
THE MONARCHS' EPIC MIGRATION

"Larka," I say, "Sammie's gone." Her tail lowers until it's at half-mast, as if in mourning. I grab her lady-in-the-circus beard, draw myself closer. I need her to understand that the world has grown smaller with the loss of her pal, Sammie, the old black lab. "Martha had to put her down. She had cancer. You had cancer, too. Do you remember?"

Larka lifts her front right paw, the one minus the cancerous big toe, as if to remind me of the Chinese philosophy she adopted after it was amputated: *who needs ten toes when nine will do?*

I take her paw, pat it, like a gloved hand. "I know, I know," I go on, "our rallying cry was *off with her toe!* and not, *off with her head!* Unlike yours, Sammie's cancer couldn't be amputated."

I give Larka a biscuit to reward her, once more, for surviving her cancer, then say, "A biscuit a day keeps the vet away. Now let's go to the beach."

Her tail goes up. Her nine toes skitter across the bamboo floor.

The dog beats me to the front door. Once in the car, we head for Sea Point beach. We drive by houses quiet as candlelight, by stone walls missing grey teeth, hand-knotted grasses. Fish-shaped leaves swim in trees umbrellaed by light while we drive under clouds puffing out their pudgy cheeks. The air coming through the windows is succulent as clarified sweet butter.

Once we get to Sea Point, Larka bounds out of the car, barking, like an oversized hare. Does she see Sammie's ghost? I can't help but scan the shoreline for Sammie's seal-like coat, all black except for the white whiskers round her square jaw. I can't help but scan the beach for Martha, tall, stoic as Amelia Earhart. I hear Martha say, *Blood in Sammie's urine. Worse things are coming.* I hear her say, *got to get myself ready, but you never can.*

We walk by the sea, listen to its mountainous uproar, big bellowy bass notes and sundering thunder. I note how it's endlessly useful, the way verbs are endlessly useful, even loss is, churning as it does in depths we can't fathom. Loss is the muscle that flexes with each step I take, the audible light that dovetails with the sundering waves, the froth they toss up, like a glassblower's breath. It's what keeps the birds aloft, not just afloat. Although their tiny bones look insufficient to the task, each wing flap says, *awe, awe.*

At the end of the long stretch of wand-shaped beach is the point itself, buffered and turreted by boulders black as stout. When the dog and I step onto its narrow trail, we brush by the crabbed, cranial skulls of Queen Anne's Lace, rose hips simmering like persimmons, chick-colored butter and eggs. We climb out on the boulders themselves, heaved there by some force greater than God's--they're crooked smokestacks, jagged top hats.

Sea spray spangles the air, as if it were fluted champagne. Because the ocean ceaselessly flowers this lutescent spray, it's monumentally festive, toasting as it does--without beginning, without end--to a force larger than itself. I toast that force, as well. I toast the gay occasion each breath of air affords, the spiritual sense coarsely ground in the sea's infinitesimal grains of salt and jellyfish floating like orange Chinese lanterns. I toast the shrapnel grace that scours away the bitter tone we oft we use with our own. My voice, its singular chorus in the beautiful all, is also clarified, like sweet butter.

I grow iambic with wonder. In wonder, I toss a dog biscuit into this ceaselessly flowering, endlessly useful sea. I toss the biscuit for Sammie. When I do, my dog almost jumps in to rescue it, even though she hates to get her nine toes wet.

As the biscuit gets churned in depths we can't fathom, I picture Sammie swimming her way to doggy heaven, not caring whether if it's here, or there. She's just happy to be swimming. In the word balloon above her head, there's a frisbee with a halo around it. Sammie loved to leap for the frisbee almost as much as Ryan does.

Although my dog thinks tossing a perfectly good biscuit into the sea is the waste of a perfectly good biscuit, this doesn't stop her from doing a happy dance for Sammie once we round the point, get back down onto the beach. First Larka rolls in flat, gold sand studded with a rainbow of starfish, then starts running around me in ever-widening circles--bunny hopping, barking and leaping all the while. She even nips my coat, something she did as a pup, nine years before. Once she leaps so high, she breezes by my right shoulder. Maybe she, too, knows how to stay aloft, not just afloat. Her ears flap like wings, *awe, awe.*

Next morning, we head down to Fort Foster to walk with the Wednesday Walkers. They are my Walky-Talkies, minus the florescent shoelaces. Us Wednesday Walkers meet at the gates to Fort Foster, not only on Wednesdays, but Monday and Fridays, too.

Marcia is there, assisting Martha, who uses a walker because she has Parkinson's Disease. Although she can't manage the seaside trail anymore, Martha does go out to the end of the pier, buoyed by us women.

I see that Sara is standing at the gate, as is Eileen, Merry, Charlotte, Kathleen, A.M. There are the dogs: Java, Jamie, Vlad, Lucky, Larka. We walk toward the pier, like a flotilla, our voices, free of the bitter tone. Bird wings flap, *awe, awe,* in an octave above heaven. We walk down the pier, noting how the water is jewel-toned in some places, opalescent mother of pearl in others. None of it, no, none, is lost on us as we mill at the end of the pier.

We embark upon the seaside trail. We walk through a stand of sumac, rounded like a bridal bower. On the other side, leaves, rocks, sky, are brilliantly displayed with hundreds upon thousands of monarch butterflies. The miraculous comes close as these monarchs alight, dazzling as orange party bows.

We look up: the monarchs soiree, lecture us on the virtues of high lyricism. The tiny machines in their bodies go *whir,* as we're plunged into a fairyland full of dancing feet--*ours!* We gape at this ever-shifting crazy quilt, this flitting rag tail collage. The dogs do their own happy dance.

As we're plunged, my own epic migration comes to its grand,

Kirschnerian finale-moving, as it does, like the fast parts of stories toward sudden, swift conclusions.

My finale is an arrival. It's to arrive here, among the Wednesday Walkers, feeling the miraculous. My finale concludes that little bits of precocious genius are tucked inside each of these monarchs, just as it's tucked into each of us. It's the voltage that turns us on, what gets all us women dancing. It's contagious as laughter, spreads like wildfire and when the monarchs, like tiny flashcards, alight and bolt, often at the same time, we know we depend on this--the audible light plunging its spears in waves, the boulders, ruddy-red as canyons and the dazzle of this epic migration, yes, we depend on all of it to deliver us, like a wild guess, from one day to the next.

Postlude: SIGHTINGS FROM SPRUCE CREEK BRIDGE

Who is that woman who comes stomping out of her little house, her Sea Cabin, morning, noon and night? Why does she come stomping out of her Sea Cabin in all weathers and seasons--in rain and bristling winds, in the season of pepper and forgetfulness, in heat, hot as a dime on tarmac, slugger winter storms emptying trousseaus of snow? She's out there in the season of seedpods and salamanders, in angers hot as frost-fire, or is it the ceaseless season we call grief?

Where do you sight this woman?

We sight her as we cross Spruce Creek Bridge. We see her stomp out of her little house in yellow wellies, wide as stovepipes, and a man's old plaid bathrobe. Her ex-husband's? She sports a lime-green shower cap bustling with fat white daisies--does she think it makes her strange appearance dapper?

This woman, who stomps out of her house, is followed by a feckless dog. She makes a beeline down to the marina, which her Sea Cabin's a part of. She beelines it down to the marina, followed by her black dog, marches out on the dock, queen bee-like, in her yellow wellies, old plaid bathrobe, lime-green shower cap. But that's only half the spectacle.

What's the other half of the spectacle?

The other half consists in watching this woman charge past the old fish shanty poised atop that dock. She charges, full steam, down the ramp. Here, the boats are moored--the angle of the ramp depends upon the tide. If it's low tide, the ramp is steep. The dog's nine toes skittishly scrape as she skitters down after her owner, who's nearly wobbling in her yellow wellies, wide as stovepipes.

What does this woman do next?

In her strange riggings, she marches to the end of the dock where she hucks things right into the river. Rumor has it that she only hucks what's most precious to her. Once she hucked an ungainly garden ornament into the river (from a crappy boyfriend?) Not only did she huck this garden ornament into the water, she did so while swearing at the top of her lungs.

What else have you seen this woman huck?

We've seen her huck a passport (her mother's?) as if it would give her transport into a universe more essential than this one. Isn't that strange? Plum cuckoo, we say.

Why she also hucked a man's silver watch (her father's?) into the river. Jewelry's been hucked--pearls, coral earrings, red as a tenderloin, a glow-in-the-dark rosary. A glow-in-the-dark rosary? What a fruitcake!

Good Lord, she even hucked her wedding ring into the river with a *fuck!* What sort of nutcase would huck her own wedding ring into the fathoms below?

We've seen books get hucked (her own?) into the water, as well as photographs, hatboxes, party lights squiggling like electric eels as they sank. Is this some sort of bizarre exorcism? Good Lord, it's time to lock her in the nuthouse and throw away the key!

We wonder: is there a priceless, if quirky archeological dig at the bottom of Spruce Creek, a sizable heap of barnacled belongings belonging only to ogle-eyed fish, sea worms, fat as thumbs, taffy-colored kelp? Should we all jump in to help ourselves?

What happens next?

This is when the most sensational moment in the entire spectacle occurs. Just after what's most precious to this woman gets hucked into the river, she does an about-face, bends over, flips up that old plaid bathrobe and moons the universe.

After mooning the universe, she uprights herself, smooths down her plaid bathrobe, as though it were a ballroom gown, then lets out a sigh of dreamy relief.

She then demurely saunters down the dock. She saunters, all lady-like, by the boats while her feckless dog, princess-like, trots behind. Up the ramp she goes, as if straight out of Charm School with a book (one of her own?) balanced atop that lime-green shower cap. She demurely heads back to her Sea Cabin, as if the spectacle we just witnessed never occurred.

Then what?

This woman disappears into her little house, closing her door with a *ta-da.* Weeks, months, will pass before such a sighting recurs. But, oh, what music we hear coming from her Sea Cabin, morning, noon and night. We hear Bach and the Blitz Kreig. We hear the dum-de-dum-da of her dead, the groan her roses clutch deep in their velvet purses and the frozen cry of a child being dragged away from her dying mother, father and brother on a hill where tents palpitated with the uneasy wheeze of death breaths.

What else do you hear?

We hear the music of her fifty-eight Octobers. We hear fifty-eight gongs on an ancient temple bell whose coppery patina is covered with roseate mosses. The sound of her fifty-eight Octobers is in the heron's cry, the ping-pong of rain bouncing on her roof. It's the roar of the sea in her solar eardrum, love cries in the lunar one and always, the heave-ho of the blood. Add to this the susurration of gull cry, the atomic rush of light and the foghorns which weep, piquantly, from her rafters.

What do you wonder about?

We wonder who the author is of this music? Do we care so long as it drifts, like boas of smoke, or tinctures of distilled honeysuckle into us, until our pores are downright dewy? We breathe in this music, like a draught of dressy breezes that have been a long time coming, or the scent of yeasty bread rising in some dank corner.

While we breathe in this dewy music, we can't help but wonder what the story is behind it all, or better yet, what the story is behind this woman herself. Some say she's a poet, and of course, such rumors elicit nothing but pity from us.

Still, how can we care whether she's a poet or not, when we're feathered with such unworldly music? Aren't we all transported into an essential universe when we're feathered with Schumann and Wallace Stevens, with Keats and Rogers and Hammerstein?

What wouldn't you object to hearing?

We wouldn't object to hearing the story behind this music, nor would we mind obliging her by listening to whatever story she might try to regale us with. After all, we can always huck *her* into the river if her story doesn't suit us, obscenities aside. We can absolutely huck her into the river in her yellow wellies, plaid bathrobe and lime-green shower cap bustling with white daisies until she, too, is part of that priceless, if quirky archeological dig.

In the end, who knows what we might find in that heap of barnacled belongings belonging only to the fish, sea worms, and taffy-colored kelp? Why not just think of it as a treasure chest buried right off Spruce Creek Bridge? Maybe her story is best told by that heap of barnacled belongings and isn't her story, our story? Aren't all stories hidden in depths we can't see, let alone fathom?

Who's to say whether her story's personal, divine, forgivable or redeeming? Isn't her story part of our larger human one and doesn't this larger one leaven us all, like yeasty bread in a dank corner, until it's broken and shared, broken and shared?

If we listen, yes listen, aren't the little voices of us all becoming something more, something greater than the separate life each body holds, than the batch of birds just now rising off of Spruce Creek? In the end, isn't the happy season here, right here, in the bright world to which she, we, thou, can, do rightly belong?

ACKNOWLEDGMENTS

Many of these chapters, in earlier versions, have been published in *THE COAL HILL REVIEW*.

I am grateful to Nancy Wheaton Modern for being the sole reader of this memoir and to Pamela Marshall, composer, and Sirarpi Heghinian Walzer, painter, for the three-way collaboration we created out of these pages to perform at The Dance Hall, Kittery, ME.

Gratitude to my son who graces my existence and to my dog, Larka Braveheart.

Sketches by Tom Rines

Author photo: Daniel Modern

Please note that some of the character's names have been changed to protect their anonymity.

ABOUT THE AUTHOR

Elizabeth Kirschner has published five volumes of poetry, most recently, *Surrender to Light, 2009,* Cherry Grove Editions and *My Life as a Doll, 2008,* Autumn House Press. *My Life as a Doll* was nominated for the Lenore Marshall Prize and named Kirschner as the Literary Arts Fellow in state of Maine in 2010. She has also published over two dozen essays with *The Coal Hill Review* and is widely published in other literary magazines, both nationally and internationally.

Most recently, Kirschner taught in Fairfield University's low-residency Program in Creative Writing. Previous teaching experience includes Boston College, Boston University and Carnegie-Mellon University.

Kirschner has collaborated with many classical composers, including Carson Cooman and Thomas Oboe Lee, resulting in various CDs. She set her own poetry to Robert Schumann's love song cycle, retitled it *The Dichterliebe in Four Seasons.* She lives in Kittery Point, ME.

Visit her at: www.elizabethkirschner.com

CPSIA information can be obtained at www.ICGtesting.com
Printed in the USA
BVOW02s0244200615

404770BV00002B/2/P